I0013166

Dark Web Unveiled

Understanding the Hidden Side of the Internet

THOMPSON CARTER

Table of Content

TABLE OF CONTENTS

INTRODUCTION

Dark Web Unveiled: Understanding the Hidden Side of the Internet

The **Dark Web** is a mysterious, complex, and often misunderstood part of the internet. While the **Surface Web**—the internet most of us interact with daily—comprises only a small fraction of the online world, the Dark Web represents an entirely different realm: an anonymous, decentralized network that exists in the shadows of the digital landscape. This book, *Dark Web Unveiled: Understanding the Hidden Side of the Internet*, aims to shed light on this hidden world, unraveling its intricacies, its implications for privacy and security, and the evolving role it plays in both legitimate and illicit activities.

The **Dark Web** has been a source of fascination and fear, often portrayed in the media as a den of illegal activity, from **drug trafficking** and **cybercrime** to **hacking** and **money laundering**. While this reputation is not without merit, the Dark Web is also a vital tool for **activists**, **journalists**, **whistleblowers**, and others who need **privacy** and **anonymity** in oppressive regimes or under surveillance. It is not simply a lawless wasteland, but a dynamic environment where both criminals and individuals seeking privacy find a space to exist outside the reach of traditional authorities.

This book will guide you through the **mysterious world** of the Dark Web, providing a **comprehensive understanding** of its structure, its uses, and its risks. We will explore the tools that enable access to the Dark Web, how criminals use it for illicit activities, and how law enforcement and cybersecurity experts are adapting to this ever-evolving landscape. Through real-world examples, this book will also offer insight into the **practical implications** of Dark Web operations—how emerging technologies like **blockchain** and **quantum computing** are reshaping the Dark Web, and what **future trends** may look like for this hidden corner of the internet.

What This Book Will Cover:

1. **Introduction to the Dark Web**: We will define the Dark Web, explain how it fits into the broader internet landscape, and explore its key characteristics, including the technology that enables its anonymity. You'll gain an understanding of the difference between the **Surface Web**, **Deep Web**, and the **Dark Web**.

2. **Navigating the Dark Web**: A practical guide to safely accessing the Dark Web, focusing on tools like **Tor** and **I2P**, and how to protect your identity and privacy while browsing. This includes tips for **avoiding scams**, **malware**, and staying **secure** in a space that thrives on **anonymity**.

3. **Dark Web Transactions**: We will dive into how blockchain technology is influencing Dark Web transactions, with a special focus on **cryptocurrencies** like **Bitcoin** and **Monero**. Learn about decentralized marketplaces, **privacy coins**, and how these technologies help maintain **financial privacy** while also enabling **illegal activities**.

4. **Criminal Activities on the Dark Web**: The Dark Web is often associated with **cybercrime**, but it's also a platform for **hackers**, **cybercriminals**, and those involved in illicit trade. We will explore how these criminals operate, the **types of crimes** facilitated on the Dark Web, and real-world examples of notorious marketplaces like **Silk Road** and **AlphaBay**.

5. **Law Enforcement on the Dark Web**: How law enforcement agencies are evolving their tactics to combat **cybercrime** on the Dark Web, including

examples of successful takedowns and the challenges they face. This section will also touch on the future of **international cooperation** and legal frameworks designed to tackle cross-border crime.

6. **Emerging Technologies**: As **artificial intelligence (AI)** and **quantum computing** continue to develop, their implications for **Dark Web encryption** and **cybersecurity** become even more significant. We will examine how these technologies may reshape the future of the Dark Web, both from the perspective of **criminals** and **law enforcement**.

7. **Protecting Yourself**: If you need to access the Dark Web for legitimate purposes, this section will provide actionable advice on how to stay **secure**, avoid risks, and ensure your **privacy** is protected. We'll discuss the best practices for securing your computer, avoiding common threats, and ensuring that you remain anonymous while navigating the Dark Web.

Why This Book Matters:

In a world where digital privacy and security are under constant threat, understanding the **Dark Web** is more important than ever. It has evolved from a tool used exclusively by **cybercriminals** to a platform for those seeking **privacy** in an increasingly surveillance-driven world. For **journalists**, **activists**, and anyone concerned about **government surveillance** or the loss of **privacy**, the Dark Web provides a refuge from the prying eyes of **authorities**, **corporations**, and other actors.

However, this same anonymity allows **cybercriminals** to exploit the Dark Web for illicit activities. As the landscape of **cybersecurity** and **digital crime** continues to shift, **law enforcement agencies** are constantly adapting to tackle emerging threats. This book will provide the **insights** you need to understand both the **opportunities** and **dangers** presented by the Dark Web, empowering you to navigate this hidden digital world securely and responsibly.

Whether you're a **researcher**, **activist**, **business professional**, or just curious about this **hidden layer** of the internet, *Dark Web Unveiled: Understanding the Hidden Side of the Internet* will give you the tools and knowledge to explore, understand, and stay **secure** while engaging with the **Dark Web**. Join us as we uncover the **mysteries** of the internet's deepest, most secretive corners.

CHAPTER 1

What is the Dark Web?

Defining the Dark Web: Understanding Its Place in the Internet Hierarchy

The **Dark Web** is a portion of the internet that is intentionally hidden from standard search engines and requires special tools to access. It's often associated with secrecy, anonymity, and activities that are difficult to trace. But the Dark Web is much more than just a place for illicit transactions; it is a complex ecosystem with both legal and illegal uses, serving various functions for people who require privacy and those engaged in criminal activities.

To fully understand the Dark Web, it's crucial to explore its place within the broader structure of the internet. The internet is often described in three layers:

1. **Surface Web**: This is the part of the internet that most people are familiar with. It consists of websites indexed by standard search engines like Google, Bing, or Yahoo. These websites are accessible by anyone with an internet connection and are visible to everyone. For example, social media platforms like

Facebook, news sites like BBC, and shopping sites like Amazon are all part of the surface web.

2. **Deep Web**: The deep web is the vast section of the internet that is not indexed by search engines. It contains pages and databases that are inaccessible through regular search engines but are not necessarily hidden. These could include private data such as email accounts, private databases, financial information, and academic repositories. For example, when you log into your email account or access a private document stored in cloud storage, you're interacting with the deep web.

3. **Dark Web**: The Dark Web is a subset of the Deep Web, but it's distinct because it's intentionally hidden and often requires specific software or configurations to access. The most common tool to access the Dark Web is **Tor** (The Onion Router), which anonymizes users by routing their traffic through multiple layers of encryption. Unlike the Deep Web, where the information is private but legitimate, the Dark Web hosts content and services that can range from legal and privacy-driven uses to illegal activities like drug trafficking, hacking services, and weapons sales.

The Dark Web exists as a place where users can operate under the radar of law enforcement, corporations, and even governments. It's often seen as a sanctuary for those who value privacy and anonymity, but it is also home to a host of illicit and illegal activities.

The Difference Between the Surface Web, Deep Web, and Dark Web

To understand the unique role of the Dark Web, it's important to differentiate it from the other two segments of the internet:

- **Surface Web**: The Surface Web, as mentioned earlier, is the portion of the internet that is visible to everyone and can be indexed by traditional search engines. This includes websites that you visit daily, such as news websites, social media platforms, and online retailers. Anything that can be found via search engines and accessed without special tools is part of the Surface Web. It's the most familiar part of the internet.

- **Deep Web**: The Deep Web comprises all the data and content that cannot be indexed by search engines. This includes databases, password-protected websites, private networks, and other content that is not meant for public consumption. The Deep Web is not illegal; it just includes pages and content that are not part of the public web. For example, academic journals that are only accessible to authorized users or internal corporate databases are part of the Deep Web. You may use the Deep Web every day without realizing it, such as when you check your bank account or read a subscription-only article.

- **Dark Web**: The Dark Web is a specialized, intentionally hidden portion of the Deep Web. It cannot be accessed by traditional browsers or search engines, and it requires specific software like **Tor** or **I2P** (Invisible Internet Project) to access. The Dark Web is often thought of as the "underground" internet because it provides a high degree of anonymity and privacy for its users. It can be a platform for legitimate uses, such as protecting privacy for journalists and activists, but it is also frequently associated with illegal activities like hacking, drug trafficking, and human trafficking.

Visualizing the Hierarchy:

- **Surface Web**: Publicly accessible and indexed by search engines.
- **Deep Web**: Includes content that is private, secure, or password-protected, but not illegal.
- **Dark Web**: A hidden subset of the Deep Web that requires specific tools for access, often associated with anonymity and illicit activity.

Real-World Example: The Case of Silk Road and Its Influence on the Dark Web

One of the most infamous examples of the Dark Web's power and influence is **Silk Road**, an online black market that operated on the Dark Web from 2011 to 2013. Silk Road became infamous for its role in facilitating the illegal trade of narcotics, fake identification, and other illicit goods, using **Bitcoin** as the primary form of payment. Silk Road was hosted on the **Tor network** and used **.onion** domains, which are only accessible via the Tor browser.

Silk Road was revolutionary in many ways:

- **Anonymity**: The platform offered a high degree of anonymity for both buyers and sellers, which was attractive to individuals looking to engage in illegal activities without being traced. The use of Tor and Bitcoin made it difficult for law enforcement to trace transactions or identify users.

- **Market for Illegal Goods**: The platform created an online marketplace for illegal goods and services that could be accessed by anyone with the right tools, making the Dark Web an infamous haven for illicit activities. Silk Road became synonymous with the idea of the Dark Web in popular culture.

- **Government Crackdown**: Silk Road was eventually shut down in 2013 by the **FBI**, and its creator, **Ross Ulbricht**, was arrested and sentenced to life in prison. The Silk Road operation highlighted the vulnerabilities and challenges of policing the Dark Web, and it sparked a global conversation about the need for law enforcement agencies to adapt to new technologies in the fight against cybercrime.

Impact of Silk Road on the Dark Web: Silk Road was not only a significant event in the history of the Dark Web, but it also played a key role in shaping its modern usage. It demonstrated the potential for anonymity on the Dark Web, but it also brought increased attention from law enforcement, which has led to greater efforts to track and shut down similar operations. Silk Road also encouraged the creation of other black markets, some of which have since been taken down as well.

Silk Road's influence is still felt today, as it proved that the Dark Web could be used to facilitate global trade in illicit goods and services. While the site is gone, the technological and social structures it helped create continue to exist on the Dark Web, and new markets have emerged to take its place.

Conclusion

The **Dark Web** is a hidden but integral part of the internet, existing below the surface of what we commonly see and access. While it often carries a negative connotation due to its association with illegal activities, it also plays a critical role in preserving privacy, enabling free speech, and offering anonymity for individuals in repressive regimes.

As we move forward in this book, we will continue to explore the various facets of the Dark Web, from its technologies to its ethical implications. Understanding the Dark Web in its entirety—both the good and the bad—is

17

essential for anyone who wants to engage with or simply understand the hidden side of the internet.

In the following chapters, we'll dive deeper into the technologies that power the Dark Web, the communities that thrive within it, and the challenges that arise from policing this hidden network. Whether you're a curious beginner or an expert seeking to broaden your understanding, this book will guide you through the complex world of the Dark Web and its ever-evolving influence on the internet.

CHAPTER 2

The Evolution of the Dark Web

A Brief History of the Dark Web

The **Dark Web** did not suddenly appear overnight, nor did it emerge solely from a desire for anonymity or secrecy. Its evolution is rooted in the need for privacy, security, and freedom of speech—fundamental principles that have driven its development, often in response to societal, political, and technological changes.

The origins of the Dark Web can be traced back to the early days of the **internet**, particularly when privacy and anonymity online became central concerns. Initially, the internet was designed as an open network with relatively few barriers to access. However, as it grew and became more integrated into everyday life, issues of **surveillance**, **data privacy**, and **censorship** began to emerge. In response to these concerns, the Dark Web evolved as a way to provide users with a place to communicate and interact in ways that could not be easily monitored or traced.

- **Early Foundations (1990s–2000s)**: In the early 1990s, the internet was largely unregulated, and users had relatively few privacy concerns. However, as the web grew, governments and corporations began to take notice, leading to concerns about the tracking of individuals and the collection of personal data. The rise of **cybersecurity** and government surveillance in the post-9/11 world pushed the demand for tools that could help users protect their identity and data.

- **The Birth of the Dark Web (2000s)**: The Dark Web began to take shape during the early 2000s with the creation of technologies aimed at offering anonymity and privacy. The pivotal moment came in **2002** with the creation of **Tor (The Onion Router)**, a network that would allow users to access the internet anonymously. As Tor matured, it became the most widely used tool for accessing the Dark Web, providing a layer of encryption that allowed users to hide their identities and activities.

- **Silk Road and the Rise of Dark Web Markets (2011)**: The launch of Silk Road in 2011 is often seen as the defining moment that brought the Dark Web into the public consciousness. Silk Road, an online marketplace for illegal goods (primarily drugs), used Tor to remain hidden from law enforcement and operated exclusively on the Dark Web. Despite its eventual shutdown in 2013, Silk Road's success demonstrated the potential for both **illegal** and **legitimate** uses of the Dark Web, such as maintaining privacy in oppressive regimes and facilitating secure communication.

- **Continued Growth and Challenges (2013–Present)**: Following the closure of Silk Road, numerous similar marketplaces appeared, often evolving into more complex and decentralized platforms. The law enforcement response to these marketplaces became more aggressive, resulting in the takedown of other large-scale operations, such as **AlphaBay** and **Hansa Market**. Despite these efforts, the Dark Web continues to grow and evolve, with new tools and techniques emerging to circumvent law enforcement and protect users.

The Technological Milestones That Made the Dark Web Possible

The Dark Web would not exist without certain key technological advancements that enabled its creation and sustained its growth. These innovations have been crucial in ensuring that users can access this hidden part of the internet while maintaining privacy and anonymity.

1. **The Development of Tor (The Onion Router)**:
    o **Tor**, originally developed by the **U.S. Navy** in the late 1990s, was designed to protect government communications from surveillance. It was built to enable the anonymous transmission of data over the internet by routing communications through multiple layers of encryption, like the layers of an onion. This system made it difficult for anyone to trace the origin of the traffic or identify the user.
    o Tor became the foundational technology for the Dark Web. It allowed websites to exist with **.onion** domains—hidden services that are only accessible through the Tor network, ensuring that both users and servers remain anonymous.

2. **The Rise of Cryptocurrencies**:
    o **Bitcoin**, created in 2009 by the pseudonymous individual or group **Satoshi Nakamoto**, revolutionized how transactions were made online. Bitcoin enabled users to make pseudonymous transactions, providing another layer of anonymity for Dark Web transactions. The integration of Bitcoin with the Dark Web led to the creation of marketplaces where users could

buy and sell goods, often illicit, while maintaining their anonymity.

o Other cryptocurrencies like **Monero**, known for its enhanced privacy features, gained popularity within Dark Web markets for providing even greater levels of transaction anonymity.

3. **Secure Communication Tools**:

o Over time, other privacy-focused tools emerged to further secure communication on the Dark Web. These include encrypted messaging platforms like **Signal** and **ProtonMail**, which have been used by individuals engaging in sensitive communications, from journalists to activists.

o These tools are often integrated into Dark Web platforms, offering a layer of confidentiality for users seeking to evade surveillance.

4. **Peer-to-Peer Networks and Decentralized Hosting**:

o Peer-to-peer (P2P) technologies and decentralized networks have played a role in ensuring the continued anonymity and resilience of the Dark Web. By decentralizing the hosting of websites and services, these technologies reduce the risks of a single point of failure.

- o **I2P (Invisible Internet Project)** is one example of a decentralized network designed to improve privacy and facilitate the Dark Web's growth. Unlike Tor, I2P is designed to allow for anonymous browsing and hosting within the network itself, making it harder for authorities to take down specific sites.

5. **Encryption and Data Protection**:
   - o The advent of **strong encryption** methods has been critical to securing communications and data on the Dark Web. Services like **PGP (Pretty Good Privacy)** encryption are widely used to protect emails and other communications on the Dark Web, allowing individuals to share sensitive information without fear of it being intercepted or compromised.
   - o Additionally, the use of **end-to-end encryption** on messaging apps and websites on the Dark Web ensures that even if data is intercepted, it remains unreadable without the proper decryption key.

Real-World Example: How the Creation of Tor Changed the Way We Think About Internet Privacy

One of the most significant turning points in the history of the Dark Web was the creation and public release of **Tor**. Tor revolutionized internet privacy by providing a free and open-source platform for anonymous browsing, bypassing traditional surveillance and censorship systems.

Tor's release in 2002 was initially intended for use by the **U.S. Navy** to protect intelligence and military communications. However, it quickly evolved into a tool used by privacy advocates, journalists, activists, and ordinary citizens who sought to protect their identities online. For example, during periods of political unrest in countries like **Iran** and **Egypt**, Tor allowed citizens to bypass state-imposed censorship and access uncensored information.

The launch of Tor allowed for the creation of **.onion** websites, which are only accessible through the Tor network. These websites are hosted anonymously, making them ideal for individuals or organizations seeking to avoid surveillance. This technology opened the doors for the **Dark**

Web to emerge as a platform for a range of activities, both legal and illegal.

Real-World Example: The case of **Ross Ulbricht** and the creation of **Silk Road** is perhaps the most well-known example of Tor's role in shaping the Dark Web. Silk Road, an online marketplace for drugs, fake identification, and other illicit items, was built on the Tor network. Ulbricht, under the pseudonym **Dread Pirate Roberts**, launched Silk Road in 2011, which quickly became a widely used platform for anonymous transactions. Despite Silk Road's eventual takedown by the FBI in 2013, the case highlighted how Tor could facilitate secure, anonymous trade, and demonstrated the broader potential of the Dark Web for both legitimate and criminal activities.

Conclusion

The **Dark Web** evolved over the course of the 21st century, driven by technological advances in anonymity, encryption, and decentralized networks. While initially developed for secure military communication, technologies like **Tor** have reshaped the internet as we know it. The Dark Web is now a platform that serves a range of users—from individuals

26

seeking privacy to criminals engaged in illicit trade. By understanding the technological milestones that made the Dark Web possible, we can begin to better understand its complexities, its role in modern society, and its potential future.

In the next chapters, we will explore the various facets of the Dark Web, including its impact on society, its uses, and the ethical and legal challenges it presents. The Dark Web is a space where privacy, freedom of expression, and cybercrime collide, and understanding its evolution is key to navigating this hidden part of the internet.

CHAPTER 3

How Does the Dark Web Work?

The Basics of Tor and I2P: Anonymous Networks that Power the Dark Web

The **Dark Web** relies on two primary technologies to ensure user anonymity and the invisibility of its content: **Tor** (The Onion Router) and **I2P** (Invisible Internet Project). These networks are designed to protect users' identities and locations, making it nearly impossible for anyone to trace their online activities.

1. Tor (The Onion Router)

Tor is the most widely used tool for accessing the Dark Web. Originally developed by the **U.S. Navy** in the 1990s to protect military communications, Tor has since evolved into a critical tool for privacy advocates, journalists, and users seeking to maintain anonymity online. It operates by encrypting and routing internet traffic through a series of **relays** (volunteer-operated servers) across the globe, creating multiple layers of encryption—hence the term **"onion" routing**.

- **How Tor Works**: When you use Tor, your internet traffic is bounced between a network of **relays**, with each relay adding another layer of encryption. This ensures that no single relay knows both the origin and destination of your data, thus making it extremely difficult for anyone to track your online activities.
  - ○ **Layered Encryption**: The "onion" metaphor comes from the way Tor encrypts your data. Just like peeling an onion, each relay removes a layer of encryption. By the time your data reaches its destination, it has passed through several layers, each of which obscures the data's origin and final destination.
  - ○ **Exit Node**: The final node in the Tor circuit is called the **exit node**. While this node decrypts the final layer of encryption and forwards the data to its destination, the origin of the data (your IP address) remains hidden from the receiving server.
- **.onion Sites**: Websites on the Dark Web typically use the **.onion** domain suffix, indicating that they are accessible only through Tor. These sites are hosted

in a way that prevents anyone from easily finding or tracking them through traditional search engines.

Benefits of Tor:

- Provides **strong anonymity** for users and websites.
- Makes it difficult for adversaries to identify the user's location or browsing activity.
- Protects against **traffic analysis** and ensures that the data remains encrypted in transit.

2. I2P (Invisible Internet Project)

I2P is another anonymous network, though it functions somewhat differently from Tor. While Tor is designed for anonymity in accessing regular websites, I2P is designed primarily for anonymous **communication** and **file sharing** within its network. It allows users to host **"hidden services"** just like Tor does, but with an emphasis on internal, peer-to-peer activity.

- **How I2P Works**: I2P also uses encryption and routing through a series of relays, but the focus is on creating **private and secure tunnels** within the I2P network. In this way, I2P is more closed off than Tor, making it harder for external parties to intercept data.

30

- o **Internal Network**: Unlike Tor, which uses exit nodes to access the regular internet, I2P is designed to operate mainly within its own network, meaning all websites hosted on I2P are accessible only from within the I2P network.

- o **Eepsites**: Websites on I2P are called **"eepsites"**, and they use the **.i2p** domain. They are accessible only to users within the I2P network, offering a higher level of privacy and anonymity.

- **Use Cases for I2P**:
  - o Ideal for users who want to host and browse content within a **peer-to-peer** environment.
  - o Often used for **secure email services**, file sharing, and other decentralized applications.

Benefits of I2P:

- Offers a **more decentralized structure** than Tor, which makes it more resistant to potential censorship or shutdown.

- Focuses on **private communication** within the network and offers strong **end-to-end encryption**.

- Used widely for **secure, peer-to-peer communications**.

Tor vs. I2P

- **Tor** is better for users who want to access the **open web** anonymously and visit **.onion** sites, while **I2P** is more focused on creating private, internal networks for file-sharing, messaging, and hosting services within the I2P ecosystem.
- **Tor** has a larger user base and is generally considered more user-friendly, while **I2P** offers more security for internal communication within its ecosystem.

How Websites and Services Are Hosted on the Dark Web

Hosting websites and services on the Dark Web is fundamentally different from hosting them on the Surface Web. On the Dark Web, **privacy**, **security**, and **anonymity** are paramount, and the hosting process incorporates several layers of encryption and hidden configurations.

1. Hosting on the Dark Web with Tor

- **Anonymous Hosting**: When setting up a website on the Dark Web, the host must ensure that the server's identity remains hidden. This is typically done by using **Tor hidden services**, where the website is hosted on a server that is also anonymized. The **.onion** domain is used to provide a unique address that can only be accessed through Tor.

- **Relaying Traffic**: When users access a **.onion** site, their traffic is routed through the Tor network, passing through multiple **Tor relays** before reaching the hidden server. This ensures that the origin and destination of the traffic are obscured, preventing attackers or surveillance agencies from identifying the server hosting the site.

- **Using Tor Hidden Services for Hosting**:
  - The website's **IP address** is hidden, and only the **.onion** address can be used to access the site.
  - Hosting a website on the Dark Web via Tor requires configuring the **Tor software** to run on the server, alongside the website's content, to ensure that all traffic remains anonymized.

- **Server Configuration**: Setting up a website on the Dark Web involves installing Tor software on the web server and configuring it to act as a **hidden service**. The web server then communicates through Tor's encrypted network, making it nearly impossible to trace the origin of the server's location.

2. Hosting on the Dark Web with I2P

- **Eepsites**: In I2P, websites are called **"eepsites"**, and they are hosted on the I2P network, not the regular internet. An eepsite can only be accessed by users who are also using I2P, and its domain ends with **.i2p**. Just like with Tor, I2P ensures that both the user and the website remain anonymous.

- **End-to-End Encryption**: Just like Tor, I2P uses **end-to-end encryption** to ensure that communications between the server and the client are private and protected from surveillance.

- **Decentralization**: Unlike Tor, which uses centralized exit nodes to reach the public internet, I2P operates more in a decentralized manner. Websites hosted on I2P are accessible only from within the I2P network, providing an additional layer of security.

Real-World Example: Accessing a .onion Site and Understanding Hidden Services

To truly understand how the Dark Web works, let's look at an example of accessing a **.onion** website using **Tor**.

1. **Installing Tor**: The first step in accessing a **.onion** site is installing the **Tor browser** on your device. The Tor browser is based on **Mozilla Firefox** and comes pre-configured to route all traffic through the Tor network.

2. **Accessing a .onion Site**: Once you've installed the Tor browser, you can type in a **.onion** address into the browser's search bar. For instance, accessing a marketplace like **The Hub Market** (a known Dark Web marketplace) requires the URL to be entered exactly as it appears, because **.onion** sites are not indexed by search engines.

3. **How Tor Routes Your Request**: When you access the **.onion** site, your request is routed through the Tor network, which encrypts and anonymizes your traffic through several relays. This makes it difficult for anyone (including the site's host) to track your identity or location.

4. **Understanding Hidden Services**: The **.onion** domain is a **hidden service**, meaning that both the server and the client remain anonymous. The web server hosting the marketplace does not know who is accessing it, and the user does not know where the

server is physically located. Only the encrypted **.onion** address allows users to access the service.

5. **Security and Privacy**: When interacting with the site, all of the communication remains encrypted. This ensures that even if someone were to intercept the traffic, they would not be able to read it or learn anything about the user or the site itself.

Real-World Use Case:

- **Whistleblowers** and journalists frequently use the Dark Web to communicate securely and anonymously. For example, the **Washington Post** uses the **SecureDrop** system, which allows whistleblowers to securely submit documents via a **.onion** site. The Tor network ensures that the identities of both the whistleblower and the journalist remain hidden, thus protecting them from government surveillance or retaliation.

Conclusion

The Dark Web, powered by technologies like **Tor** and **I2P**, offers a space for anonymous communication and hosting. These networks enable users to access websites, services, and marketplaces that cannot be traced or monitored easily, providing a level of privacy that the Surface Web cannot offer. However, while these technologies can be used for legitimate purposes such as protecting privacy, they can also be exploited for illicit activities.

In the following chapters, we will continue to explore the functionalities of the Dark Web, its uses, and its ethical and legal implications. Understanding how Tor and I2P work is key to understanding how the Dark Web operates and how it is able to maintain such a high degree of anonymity and privacy.

CHAPTER 4

Exploring the Structure of the Dark Web

How Content is Organized on the Dark Web

The **Dark Web** operates in a way that is distinctly different from the traditional **Surface Web**. Its structure is decentralized and highly anonymized, which makes it a unique and often misunderstood part of the internet. While the Surface Web is organized using traditional indexing methods that rely on search engines like Google, the Dark Web's content is hidden and often organized through specialized tools and technologies such as **Tor** and **I2P**.

The content on the Dark Web is structured around several core features that prioritize **anonymity**, **privacy**, and **security**:

1. Hidden Services

One of the defining characteristics of the Dark Web is its use of **hidden services**, which are websites that are only accessible through specific tools, such as the **Tor browser**. These websites are not indexed by traditional search engines, and their **.onion** domain is a key feature of the structure of the Dark Web. Hidden services are primarily designed to ensure that users and website operators can remain anonymous.

- **.onion Sites**: Websites on the Dark Web that end with the **.onion** extension are only accessible through Tor. These sites are specifically designed for the privacy and anonymity of their users. The **.onion** domain is a unique identifier within the Tor network, ensuring that the site's IP address and location remain hidden.

- **I2P Sites**: Similarly, websites hosted on the **I2P network** have the **.i2p** domain and are only accessible by users within the I2P ecosystem. These sites are less common than **.onion** sites but are still widely used for privacy-focused communications and activities.

2. Decentralized Hosting

Unlike the Surface Web, where content is usually hosted on centralized servers that can be traced back to a specific location or entity, the Dark Web makes use of decentralized hosting solutions. Websites are typically hosted on servers that are anonymized through **Tor's hidden services** or **I2P**. These decentralized hosting methods make it difficult for law enforcement and other third parties to locate and shut down Dark Web services.

- **Tor Hidden Services**: These are the most common form of hosting on the Dark Web. To set up a Tor hidden service, the host must configure a **hidden service descriptor** that is shared through Tor's distributed network. Once configured, the server is anonymized, and its content is accessible only through the Tor network.

- **I2P Hosting**: Websites within I2P are hosted in a similar way, focusing on keeping the hosting server's identity and location anonymous. However, unlike Tor, I2P is primarily designed for internal, decentralized communication within the I2P network.

3. Anonymity and Encryption

All content on the Dark Web is accessed with a strong emphasis on **anonymity** and **encryption**. Both the server and the client (user) are shielded from surveillance by routing data through multiple layers of encryption and relays. This ensures that the identity and location of both the website operator and the website visitor are kept private.

- **End-to-End Encryption**: Many services on the Dark Web, especially those offering communication or file-sharing capabilities, use **end-to-end encryption** to protect data from being intercepted. This encryption ensures that only the intended recipient of the data can read or access it.
- **Pseudonymity**: Dark Web users often create pseudonymous identities (aliases) to protect their real-life identity, enabling them to participate in various activities—legal or illegal—without revealing their personal details.

Common Websites and Services You'll Find on the Dark Web

The Dark Web is diverse, with a wide range of services and content that cater to both legitimate and illicit purposes. Some of the most common types of websites and services you will find on the Dark Web include:

1. Anonymous Marketplaces

One of the most well-known uses of the Dark Web is for **online marketplaces**, which often deal in **illegal goods and services**. These markets typically use **cryptocurrency** for payments to maintain the anonymity of transactions.

- **Marketplaces for Illicit Goods**: Historically, these marketplaces have been notorious for the sale of drugs, weapons, counterfeit documents, and other illegal items. **Silk Road**, which was shut down by the FBI in 2013, is the most famous example of such a marketplace.

- **Legal Goods and Services**: While the Dark Web is often associated with illegal activities, there are also markets for **legal goods** such as privacy-enhancing software, encrypted communication tools, and cryptocurrency services.

2. Forums and Communities

The Dark Web hosts various **forums and communities** that focus on a wide range of topics, from **privacy advocacy** and **whistleblowing** to **hacking** and **cybercrime**.

- **Privacy-Focused Forums**: There are forums dedicated to discussing encryption, security, and methods for protecting personal privacy. Many users come to these forums for guidance on how to protect themselves from government surveillance or corporate data collection.

- **Hacker Forums**: These forums often serve as meeting places for cybercriminals to share hacking techniques, malware, and exploit tools. Although many of these forums are illegal, some users visit them to learn about cybersecurity and ethical hacking.

3. Whistleblowing Platforms

The Dark Web has been a crucial tool for **whistleblowers**, journalists, and activists who wish to share sensitive information without exposing themselves to retaliation. Secure platforms like **SecureDrop** allow whistleblowers to submit information anonymously to journalists.

- **WikiLeaks**: Although it operates on the Surface Web, **WikiLeaks** began as a Dark Web platform. It uses the Dark Web to ensure the anonymity of sources who leak information.

4. Encrypted Email and Messaging Services

Many of the services on the Dark Web are dedicated to providing **secure communication** options for those who wish to remain anonymous. Encrypted messaging platforms allow users to communicate without the risk of government surveillance or corporate data mining.

- **ProtonMail** and **Tutanota** are well-known examples of secure email providers, but Dark Web versions of these services often take additional steps to ensure anonymity.

5. File Sharing and Data Hosting

On the Dark Web, you'll also find **file-sharing** services that enable users to share documents and media anonymously. These services are often used by activists, whistleblowers, and researchers to safely distribute confidential materials.

- **Secure File Hosting**: Sites on the Dark Web offer encrypted file storage solutions, allowing users to upload and download documents securely.

Real-World Example: Navigating the Most Popular Dark Web Markets

Let's take a deeper look at one of the most infamous Dark Web markets: **AlphaBay**. Before it was seized and shut down by law enforcement in 2017, AlphaBay was the largest and most popular market on the Dark Web, with over 200,000 users and 40,000 listings. It operated on the **Tor network** and facilitated the anonymous trade of illicit goods, such as drugs, firearms, stolen credit card data, and fake IDs.

How AlphaBay Worked:

- **Accessing the Market**: AlphaBay could only be accessed through the **Tor browser** via a **.onion** address. Once users installed Tor and configured their browsers, they could visit the marketplace, where they could search for goods, communicate with vendors, and make anonymous purchases.

- **Payment Methods**: AlphaBay used **Bitcoin** and other cryptocurrencies as its primary payment methods, ensuring that transactions were pseudonymous and difficult to trace. In some cases, users could also use **Monero**, a privacy-focused cryptocurrency that enhances anonymity even further.

- **Escrow System**: To protect buyers and sellers, AlphaBay offered an **escrow system**. When a buyer made a purchase, the payment was held in escrow until the product was delivered. If there was a dispute, the system would resolve it by considering the evidence from both parties.

- **Security and Anonymity**: AlphaBay was designed to ensure both vendors and buyers could engage in transactions without revealing their identities. The site had built-in **encryption** and used **PGP encryption** for messaging between buyers and sellers, ensuring that communications were secure.

Despite its success, AlphaBay's operation came to an end in 2017 when it was taken down by an international law enforcement operation. This marked the end of one of the largest and most popular Dark Web marketplaces. However, even after its shutdown, other marketplaces emerged to take its place, continuing the cycle of the Dark Web's hidden economy.

Real-World Impact: The rise and fall of AlphaBay illustrate how the Dark Web operates as a parallel marketplace with its own rules and technologies. While most of the market's activity was illicit, it also demonstrated how users could find privacy and anonymity online. AlphaBay's closure highlighted the ongoing battle between law enforcement agencies and the operators of Dark Web platforms.

Conclusion

The structure of the Dark Web is unique, with content and services organized around privacy, anonymity, and security. From hidden services to decentralized hosting, the Dark Web offers a completely different experience compared to the Surface Web. The most common services found on the Dark Web include **marketplaces, forums, whistleblowing platforms**, and **secure communication services**.

Navigating these markets and platforms requires special tools, like the **Tor browser** or **I2P**, which provide the necessary anonymity for both users and websites. While the Dark Web is home to illegal activity, it also serves as an essential resource for privacy-focused individuals and organizations, such as journalists and activists.

47

In the next chapters, we will continue exploring the Dark Web's use cases, security risks, and ethical considerations. Understanding the structure of the Dark Web is crucial for anyone who wishes to engage with or understand this hidden side of the internet.

CHAPTER 5

The Role of Encryption and Anonymity

How Encryption Ensures Privacy on the Dark Web

One of the foundational principles that underpin the **Dark Web** is **encryption**—the process of converting data into a form that can only be understood by someone with the correct decryption key. Encryption is critical to maintaining **privacy**, protecting **user identity**, and ensuring that **communications** remain confidential.

On the Dark Web, encryption serves several important functions:

1. Protecting Data from Surveillance

The Dark Web, by its very nature, is a space where individuals often seek to hide their identities and online activities. Encryption ensures that their actions and communications remain hidden from potential surveillance, including governmental monitoring, corporate tracking, or even malicious actors. Without encryption, any data exchanged on the internet is vulnerable to interception and exploitation.

- **End-to-End Encryption**: This is a method used on the Dark Web to ensure that only the intended recipient can read the content of a communication. Whether it's a message, file, or browsing session, **end-to-end encryption** ensures that even if the data is intercepted while in transit, it cannot be read by anyone other than the intended recipient. Popular platforms on the Dark Web, like **SecureDrop** or **ProtonMail**, use end-to-end encryption for secure communication.
- **TLS/SSL Encryption**: On the Dark Web, websites (particularly **.onion** sites) use **Transport Layer Security (TLS)** or **Secure Sockets Layer (SSL)** encryption to ensure that communication between users and the site is secure. This prevents third parties from intercepting sensitive information like login credentials, financial transactions, or personal data.

2. Ensuring Data Integrity

Encryption not only protects the confidentiality of data but also its **integrity**. By using techniques like **hashing**,

50

encrypted data is marked with a unique identifier, ensuring that it has not been tampered with during transmission.

- **Digital Signatures**: Many websites and services on the Dark Web employ **digital signatures** to ensure that the data received by a user is the same as the data that was sent. These signatures can verify the authenticity of the source and ensure that no modifications have been made to the data in transit.

3. Enabling Anonymous Payments

For **transactions** on the Dark Web—especially those involving illicit goods or services—**cryptocurrencies** like **Bitcoin** or **Monero** are often used. These cryptocurrencies are encrypted in a way that hides the identities of the sender and receiver, offering a level of anonymity in financial exchanges.

- **Bitcoin**: While Bitcoin is not entirely anonymous, it provides a pseudonymous form of payment where the identity of the user is not immediately linked to the transactions. However, advanced users and darknet markets often prefer **Monero** for its superior privacy features, such as **Ring Signatures** and **Stealth Addresses**, which further enhance transaction anonymity.

The Importance of Anonymity Tools Like Tor

While encryption plays a vital role in securing data, **anonymity tools** like **Tor** are equally essential in maintaining the privacy of users navigating the Dark Web. These tools are designed to protect a user's identity and location, preventing anyone from tracking their online behavior or tracing their activities back to their physical location.

1. How Tor Works to Ensure Anonymity

Tor (The Onion Router) is the most popular anonymity tool used on the Dark Web, enabling users to browse the internet anonymously and access hidden services (like **.onion** sites) that are otherwise inaccessible via regular browsers.

- **Layered Encryption and Relays**: When a user accesses the Dark Web through Tor, their internet traffic is routed through a network of **Tor relays**. Each relay encrypts the data, adding a layer of encryption to protect the user's identity and location. This process is known as **onion routing**, where each relay decrypts only a layer of the data, ensuring that no single relay knows both the origin and destination of the traffic.

- **Exit Nodes and Anonymity**: The final relay in the Tor network is called the **exit node**. While the exit node decrypts the final layer of encryption and sends the data to its destination, it cannot trace the request back to the original user. This multi-layered, decentralized system ensures that users remain anonymous and their activities are hidden from external observers, including law enforcement and hackers.

- **Accessing .onion Websites**: When users visit websites on the Dark Web, the sites have **.onion** domain extensions, which can only be accessed via Tor. These sites are hosted anonymously, and the location of the server is obscured from both the user and anyone attempting to monitor the traffic. This allows individuals to host content on the Dark Web without revealing their identity or the location of their servers.

2. The Role of Tor in Circumventing Censorship

Tor is also widely used by individuals living under repressive regimes or in countries where internet access is heavily censored. Tor allows users to access restricted websites, social media platforms, and other uncensored content without fear of government surveillance.

- **Bypassing Government Surveillance**: In countries like China, where internet censorship is prevalent, Tor is used by individuals and journalists to access uncensored information. Tor provides a means of bypassing firewalls and network filtering systems, offering a lifeline to individuals trying to access free and open information in an otherwise restricted environment.

- **Whistleblowing and Freedom of Speech**: Tor has become a critical tool for **whistleblowers** and **activists** in countries with authoritarian governments. Platforms like **SecureDrop** allow whistleblowers to anonymously leak documents and sensitive information to journalists, helping expose government corruption or human rights abuses.

3. Tor vs. VPN: What's the Difference?

While both **Virtual Private Networks (VPNs)** and **Tor** provide a degree of privacy, they differ significantly in how they ensure anonymity:

- **VPN**: A VPN can hide your IP address by routing your traffic through a server located in a different region, making it appear as though you are accessing the internet from a different location. However, VPNs are typically **centralized** and the VPN provider could potentially monitor or log your activity.

- **Tor**: Tor, on the other hand, is **decentralized**, meaning that no single entity controls the network or has access to the traffic. Tor also provides **multiple layers of encryption**, ensuring that your activities are far more difficult to trace than with a VPN.

While VPNs are useful for general privacy and security, Tor is considered far more effective when it comes to maintaining **true anonymity** on the Dark Web.

Real-World Example: Why Journalists and Activists Rely on the Dark Web for Secure Communication

One of the most important real-world uses of the Dark Web, especially for individuals concerned about their safety and privacy, is its role in **secure communication**. Journalists, activists, and whistleblowers often rely on the Dark Web to communicate securely, protect their identities, and safely leak sensitive information without fear of retaliation or surveillance.

Example 1: The Role of SecureDrop for Whistleblowers

SecureDrop is a platform designed to allow whistleblowers to submit documents to journalists anonymously and securely. It's hosted on the Dark Web (via Tor) to ensure that both the whistleblower and the journalist remain **anonymous**.

- **How It Works**: Journalists set up SecureDrop on their own Tor-enabled servers, creating a **.onion** site that is accessible only via Tor. Whistleblowers who have information they wish to leak can visit the site, upload documents, and communicate with the journalist without revealing their identity or location.
- **Privacy and Protection**: The use of Tor ensures that the identity of the whistleblower is hidden, preventing any risks associated with revealing their true identity. Additionally, SecureDrop uses **end-to-end encryption** to protect the data during transmission, ensuring that any information shared remains confidential.

- **Global Use**: SecureDrop is used by major news organizations, including **The Washington Post**, **The Guardian**, and **The New York Times**, to facilitate secure communication with whistleblowers worldwide. The ability to share sensitive documents and information anonymously has been instrumental in exposing government corruption, corporate wrongdoing, and other human rights violations.

Example 2: Journalists Reporting in Repressive Regimes

In countries where journalists and activists face threats of surveillance, arrest, or violence, the Dark Web offers a safe space to communicate, report, and expose information. For example:

- **Journalists in China**: Journalists in China have used Tor to bypass the **Great Firewall** and access censored content. They can also communicate securely with sources outside the country to gather information that might otherwise be suppressed by the government.
- **Activists in the Middle East**: During times of political unrest, such as the **Arab Spring**, activists used Tor to organize protests and share information with international media outlets without revealing their identities.

Conclusion

Encryption and **anonymity** are the cornerstones of the Dark Web's ability to protect users from surveillance and data breaches. The use of tools like **Tor** and **I2P** ensures that individuals can browse the internet and communicate securely without fear of being tracked or censored. Encryption not only protects data from interception but also ensures that online interactions remain private and untraceable.

The role of Tor, in particular, cannot be overstated, as it provides a mechanism for users to navigate the Dark Web anonymously and securely, bypassing censorship and protecting their privacy. Real-world examples, such as **journalists** and **activists** using the Dark Web for secure communication, highlight the vital role it plays in safeguarding **freedom of speech**, **whistleblowing**, and the **exchange of sensitive information** in environments where privacy is under constant threat.

As we continue exploring the Dark Web, it is essential to understand the tools that make anonymity and privacy possible, and how they shape the way people use this hidden side of the internet.

CHAPTER 6

The Tor Network and Its Importance

The Technology that Powers Tor

At the heart of the **Dark Web** lies **Tor** (The Onion Router), a technology that enables users to browse the internet anonymously and access hidden services. Tor is a **decentralized** network that uses **onion routing** to encrypt and anonymize internet traffic, ensuring that users' online activities are shielded from surveillance and tracking.

1. Onion Routing

The core technology behind Tor is called **onion routing**, a method of transmitting internet traffic through multiple layers of encryption. Each piece of data sent through the Tor network is encrypted multiple times, like the layers of an onion. This process involves passing the data through several **relays** (volunteer-run servers), each of which decrypts one layer of the data before passing it along to the next relay.

- **Multi-layered Encryption**: When a user sends a request through Tor, the data is encrypted in a way that each relay can only decrypt one layer of encryption. This ensures that no single relay knows both the origin and the destination of the data, thus providing strong anonymity.

- **Relay Structure**: The network consists of three types of relays:

  1. **Entry Node**: The first relay that receives the user's traffic and removes the first layer of encryption. It knows the user's IP address but not the destination.

  2. **Middle Node**: This relay serves as an intermediary that routes the data to the next node, adding another layer of protection.

  3. **Exit Node**: The final relay in the network, which decrypts the last layer of encryption and sends the data to its final destination (such as a website). The exit node knows the destination but not the source.

By routing data through multiple relays and applying layers of encryption at each step, Tor ensures that no single relay knows the entire path of the data, making it nearly impossible to trace the source or destination.

2. Hidden Services (Onion Sites)

One of the key features of Tor is the ability to host **hidden services**, which are websites or services that are only accessible through the Tor network. These hidden services are often referred to as **.onion sites**.

- **.onion Domains**: Websites that are hosted on the Tor network use the **.onion** extension, which is different from standard domain names (.com, .org, etc.). These sites are not indexed by traditional search engines, and their IP addresses are hidden.

- **Hosting Anonymous Websites**: Tor allows website operators to host services in such a way that their physical location is concealed. The server that hosts the website communicates through the Tor network, ensuring that it cannot be traced or identified. This is a crucial aspect of the Dark Web, where users and website owners prioritize privacy.

How Tor Achieves Anonymity and the Role It Plays in the Dark Web

Tor's role in providing anonymity and enabling the **Dark Web** cannot be overstated. While encryption ensures the privacy of data, Tor goes a step further by also masking users' **identities** and **locations**, making it extremely difficult for anyone to trace their online activity.

1. Anonymity for Users

One of the most significant features of Tor is its ability to anonymize users, preventing websites and third parties from identifying or tracking them.

- **Hiding User Identity**: When you use Tor, your **IP address** (which typically reveals your physical location) is hidden, and your browsing activity is encrypted. Websites you visit can only see the **exit node**'s IP address, not your real IP address, making it nearly impossible for anyone (including the website operator) to trace your activities back to you.
- **Bypassing Geo-blocking**: Because your internet traffic passes through multiple relays located in various regions, Tor allows you to **circumvent geo-restrictions** and access content from anywhere in the world. For instance, if a website is only accessible in the United States, you can route your traffic through a U.S.-based relay to appear as if you're browsing from there.

2. Protecting Against Traffic Analysis

Tor is also designed to protect users from **traffic analysis**, a technique used to monitor and analyze internet traffic patterns in order to identify the source, destination, or type of activity.

- **Unpredictable Routing**: The randomization of traffic routes within the Tor network makes it extremely difficult for adversaries to conduct traffic analysis. Because each user's data passes through different relays, and the number of hops (relays) can vary, tracking patterns becomes highly complex.

- **Decentralized Structure**: Tor's decentralized nature means that no single entity controls the network. This is vital in preventing any party, such as an Internet Service Provider (ISP) or government, from gaining enough information to link user activity to a specific person.

3. Role in the Dark Web

Tor is the primary tool that enables users to access the **Dark Web** and the **hidden services** hosted there. The **.onion** domain is exclusive to Tor, and it is where the bulk of Dark Web content is hosted.

- **Dark Web Marketplaces**: A significant portion of the Dark Web is made up of **illicit marketplaces** that facilitate the exchange of drugs, weapons, counterfeit documents, and other illegal goods. These sites use Tor's encryption and anonymity to protect the identity of both buyers and sellers, making it difficult for authorities to track transactions.

- **Whistleblowing Platforms**: Tor is used by platforms like **SecureDrop** to facilitate secure communication between journalists and whistleblowers. These platforms provide a means for individuals to anonymously leak sensitive information, such as government secrets or corporate malfeasance, without fear of retribution.

- **Political Activism**: In countries with heavy surveillance or censorship (e.g., China, Iran), Tor provides a way for individuals to access uncensored information, communicate freely, and bypass government censorship.

Real-World Example: How Tor Helps Users in Repressive Regimes Avoid Surveillance

In countries where freedom of expression is restricted, and government surveillance is rampant, Tor provides a **critical lifeline** for individuals seeking to access the free internet without risking their safety.

Example 1: Journalists in Authoritarian Countries

In **China**, for example, where the government maintains strict control over internet access and censors information, Tor has been used by journalists and human rights activists to circumvent the **Great Firewall**—China's internet censorship system. Tor allows users in China to access websites and platforms that would otherwise be blocked, including news outlets, social media platforms, and international resources.

- **Journalistic Integrity**: In authoritarian regimes, journalists often face persecution for publishing content critical of the government. Tor allows them to communicate securely with sources and transmit information without fear of being tracked. In 2011, the **BBC** even partnered with Tor to provide a secure method for citizens in China to access BBC content without censorship.

Example 2: Activists During Political Unrest

During periods of **political unrest**—such as the **Arab Spring** in 2011—activists in countries like **Egypt**, **Tunisia**, and **Syria** turned to Tor to organize protests, disseminate information, and avoid government surveillance. In these instances, Tor helped bypass government-imposed internet shutdowns and ensured that citizens could continue to communicate despite heavy restrictions.

- **Bypassing Censorship**: In 2011, when internet access was cut off during protests in Egypt, activists used Tor to continue organizing and sharing critical information about the protests. Tor's ability to evade censorship and surveillance played a crucial role in helping protesters maintain communication with the outside world.

- **Protection from Retaliation**: In many cases, activists who participated in protests faced violence or imprisonment. Tor provided them with a way to express their opinions and participate in political movements without revealing their identity or location, protecting them from government retaliation.

Example 3: Whistleblowers

Whistleblowers, like those who have revealed government corruption or corporate malfeasance, also rely on Tor to protect their identities while leaking sensitive documents. Platforms like **WikiLeaks** and **SecureDrop** offer anonymous communication channels that allow whistleblowers to share documents with journalists securely.

- **The Case of Edward Snowden**: In 2013, Edward Snowden, a former NSA contractor, used Tor to communicate with journalists from **The Guardian** and **The Washington Post** while leaking classified information about global surveillance programs. Snowden's case highlights the importance of Tor in providing anonymity to individuals who expose governmental wrongdoing.

Conclusion

Tor plays an essential role in providing anonymity, privacy, and security to users on the Dark Web. By using **onion**

routing and encryption, Tor ensures that both users and website hosts can browse, communicate, and interact without revealing their identities or locations. Its decentralized nature and strong encryption make it an indispensable tool for privacy-conscious individuals and organizations, especially in repressive regimes where free expression is under threat.

Whether used by journalists in authoritarian countries, activists during political unrest, or whistleblowers leaking sensitive documents, Tor has proven to be a vital tool for maintaining **freedom of speech**, **privacy**, and **security** in an increasingly surveillance-driven world.

As we continue to explore the technologies and operations of the Dark Web, we will see how Tor serves as the backbone of this hidden internet, providing access to both legitimate and illicit services while ensuring that privacy remains at the forefront of its design.

CHAPTER 7

I2P and Other Anonymity Tools

An Introduction to I2P and Its Comparison to Tor

While **Tor** is the most popular and widely used tool for accessing the **Dark Web**, **I2P** (Invisible Internet Project) is another important anonymity network that serves a similar purpose but with a different structure and approach. Both Tor and I2P are designed to provide users with privacy, anonymity, and secure communication, but they operate in distinct ways and cater to slightly different needs.

1. What is I2P?

I2P is an anonymous **overlay network** that provides users with privacy and anonymity by encrypting their internet traffic and routing it through a series of **relays**. Like Tor, I2P allows users to access both the **Surface Web** and the **Dark Web** securely. However, I2P is primarily designed for **peer-to-peer** communication and **internal web services** within the I2P network, making it distinct from Tor, which is optimized for anonymous browsing of the **Surface Web** and access to **.onion** websites.

- **Purpose**: I2P is focused on allowing anonymous **communications** between users, particularly for activities like file sharing, messaging, and hosting hidden services (called **"eepsites"**).

- **Decentralized Structure**: I2P is more decentralized than Tor, and it allows users to set up services within the network. While Tor provides access to the regular internet via its **.onion** sites, I2P focuses on internal networking where all participants are part of the I2P network.

2. Key Differences Between Tor and I2P

While both Tor and I2P have a similar goal of maintaining **anonymity**, their design and functionality differ significantly.

- **Purpose and Use Case**:
  - o **Tor** is primarily designed for anonymous **browsing** of the Surface Web and for accessing hidden services, like **.onion** websites on the Dark Web. It is widely used by individuals who want to browse the regular internet anonymously or access **Tor-hidden services**.
  - o **I2P**, on the other hand, is more focused on providing **secure, private, and anonymous**

communications within the **I2P network**. I2P is better suited for **internal networks**, where both the users and the services they interact with are also using I2P.

- **Traffic Routing**:
  - **Tor** routes data through a series of **three relays** (entry, middle, and exit) that each add a layer of encryption. The exit node decrypts the last layer and sends data to its destination.
  - **I2P** routes data through **multiple hops** within the I2P network, which is specifically designed to keep all communications **within the I2P ecosystem**. It's much more difficult to access the regular internet via I2P, as it's mostly used for **internal services**.

- **Performance**:
  - **Tor** tends to have slower browsing speeds due to the **multiple layers of encryption** and routing through relays around the world. It is optimized for access to the **Surface Web** and **.onion** sites.
  - **I2P** can also be slow but tends to perform better for **peer-to-peer communication** and **file sharing** within its own network, especially for services like **anonymous email** and **file storage**.

- **Hidden Services**:

- Tor supports **.onion** sites, allowing users to host **hidden services** that are publicly accessible to others using Tor.
- **I2P** uses the **.i2p** domain for hosting **eepsites**, but unlike Tor, these sites are not designed for access from the Surface Web. All visitors to an **eepsite** must be using I2P as well, ensuring that the entire system remains within the I2P network.

3. How I2P Works

I2P functions by encrypting data and routing it through multiple **hops** within the I2P network. When users access I2P, their data is first encrypted and passed through a **series of relays** (known as **routers**). Unlike Tor, where the exit node sends data to the destination server on the regular internet, I2P routes traffic entirely within the I2P network.

- **Anonymous Messaging**: I2P provides **anonymous messaging services** where users can communicate without revealing their identity or location.
- **File Sharing**: I2P supports file-sharing services within its network, often used for **torrenting** or **anonymous file transfers**.
- **Internal Hosting**: Websites hosted on I2P are **internal**, meaning they cannot be accessed from the

regular internet. Users must have I2P installed to access **.i2p** sites.

Exploring Other Tools for Accessing the Dark Web

While Tor and I2P are the two most popular anonymity networks, there are several other tools and technologies designed to help users maintain privacy and access the Dark Web securely. These tools often serve specific purposes or cater to different privacy needs.

1. VPN (Virtual Private Network)

A **VPN** is another tool that can help users maintain their privacy while accessing the Dark Web. While it doesn't provide the same level of anonymity as Tor or I2P, a VPN can **encrypt** users' internet traffic and route it through a secure server, hiding their IP address and location.

- **How It Works**: When you use a VPN, your internet traffic is sent through an encrypted tunnel to a remote server. This hides your IP address from websites and services, providing some degree of anonymity. However, a VPN doesn't mask the origin of your traffic as thoroughly as Tor does, and the VPN provider could potentially log or track your activity.

- **Limitations**: While a VPN can provide **anonymity** and **privacy** when browsing the Surface Web or accessing the Dark Web, it does not protect users from **traffic analysis** or provide access to **hidden services** like Tor does.

2. Freenet

Freenet is another **decentralized** network designed to provide anonymous communication and file sharing. It operates similarly to I2P in that it focuses on creating a **peer-to-peer** network where users can host and access content without revealing their identities.

- **How Freenet Works**: Freenet allows users to publish websites, blogs, and files in an **anonymous** and **decentralized** manner. Unlike Tor, Freenet does not route traffic through relays; instead, it uses **distributed data storage** to store content across the network.
- **Use Cases**: Freenet is often used by **activists** and **whistleblowers** to publish sensitive material without

revealing their identities or locations. It's also used by people in repressive regions to bypass censorship.

3. Shadowsocks

Shadowsocks is a proxy service designed to help users bypass internet censorship and access restricted content. Though it's primarily used in **China** to circumvent the **Great Firewall**, it's also used by individuals to access the Dark Web.

- **How It Works**: Shadowsocks creates an encrypted proxy between the user and the internet, allowing them to bypass restrictions and maintain some degree of privacy. It's faster than Tor but doesn't offer the same level of anonymity since it relies on a centralized proxy server.
- **Use Cases**: Shadowsocks is popular in areas with heavy internet censorship, but it's not as well-suited for accessing **.onion** sites or Dark Web content as Tor or I2P.

Real-World Example: Why Some Users Prefer I2P Over Tor for Specific Dark Web Activities

While **Tor** is often the first choice for users accessing the Dark Web, some individuals prefer **I2P** for specific activities due to its unique features, particularly for **peer-to-peer** communications and **internal services**. Below is a real-world example that illustrates why some users might choose I2P over Tor:

Example 1: File Sharing and P2P Communication

- **P2P Networks**: I2P's decentralized, peer-to-peer network is often favored by users who want to share files anonymously within the I2P network. Platforms like **I2P-Bote** (an anonymous email service) and **I2P Torrent** (a file-sharing platform) make use of I2P's **P2P** infrastructure for secure communication and file distribution.

- **Reason for Preference**: Users who engage in **file sharing** or **torrenting** within the Dark Web may prefer I2P because it is specifically designed for these types of activities, whereas Tor is not optimized for **high-bandwidth** tasks like P2P sharing.

Example 2: Hosting Internal Services

- **Internal Hidden Services**: Another reason users may prefer I2P is that it is designed for **internal hidden services**. I2P allows users to host **"eepsites"** that are only accessible to other I2P users. Unlike Tor, which allows users to access both hidden services and the Surface Web, I2P is more focused on creating a **secure, private** network that does not connect directly to the regular internet.

- **Reason for Preference**: For users who want to host websites or services that are fully contained within a **private network**, I2P offers a more suitable environment. This ensures that all traffic remains **within the I2P ecosystem**, providing additional security and protection from external surveillance.

Conclusion

Both **Tor** and **I2P** play critical roles in providing users with the anonymity and privacy needed to navigate the Dark Web securely. While **Tor** is optimized for accessing both **hidden services** and the **Surface Web**, **I2P** is more specialized in providing anonymous **peer-to-peer communication** and hosting **internal services** within its decentralized network.

Other tools, like **VPNs, Freenet**, and **Shadowsocks**, also contribute to online privacy and security, but they are generally not as suited for accessing Dark Web content or offering the same level of anonymity and encryption as Tor and I2P.

Choosing between Tor and I2P largely depends on the user's needs. For anonymous browsing of the **Surface Web** and access to **.onion sites**, Tor is the go-to solution. However, for users who need to engage in **anonymous file sharing**, **internal web services**, or **peer-to-peer activities**, I2P offers a specialized environment with enhanced privacy features.

As we continue to explore the Dark Web in this book, understanding the technologies behind Tor and I2P—and how they differ—will provide you with the tools needed to safely and securely navigate this hidden part of the internet.

CHAPTER 8

Cryptocurrencies and Payments on the Dark Web

The Role of Cryptocurrency in Dark Web Transactions

Cryptocurrency plays a pivotal role in **Dark Web transactions** due to its **anonymity**, **decentralization**, and **secure nature**, making it ideal for users who wish to engage in financial transactions without revealing their identities or locations. Unlike traditional currency, which is tied to a specific government and financial system, cryptocurrency operates on a **peer-to-peer network** and allows for **pseudonymous transactions**, meaning that users can make purchases and payments without directly linking them to their personal identity.

The benefits of using cryptocurrencies in the Dark Web are numerous:

1. Anonymity and Privacy

Cryptocurrencies, especially **Bitcoin** and **Monero**, allow users to make transactions without revealing their **real identities**. This is crucial for those who wish to protect their personal information from surveillance or law enforcement agencies. While **Bitcoin** offers a degree of anonymity, its transactions can still be traced through the **blockchain** (a public ledger), meaning that the identity of a user can potentially be uncovered if additional information is available.

On the other hand, **Monero** provides much **stronger privacy** features by employing **ring signatures** and **stealth addresses**, making it nearly impossible to trace the sender, receiver, or transaction amount.

2. Decentralization and Censorship Resistance

Unlike traditional currencies, which are controlled by governments and financial institutions, cryptocurrencies are decentralized and not subject to **central authority**. This means that no single entity can control, freeze, or censor transactions. This decentralization is particularly appealing for those operating on the Dark Web, where activities may often involve illicit goods and services that would be subject to government restrictions in traditional financial systems.

3. Security and Immutability

Cryptocurrency transactions are secured using **cryptography** and recorded on the **blockchain**, a **distributed ledger** that ensures transaction integrity. Once a transaction is confirmed and added to the blockchain, it cannot be altered or reversed. This feature of **immutability** is vital for both buyers and sellers, as it ensures that payments are final and that both parties are held accountable for their actions.

How Cryptocurrencies Like Bitcoin and Monero Are Used

Cryptocurrencies are the preferred payment method for most transactions on the Dark Web, whether the purchases are **legal** (such as privacy tools, encrypted communication services, or digital goods) or **illicit** (such as drugs, weapons, or stolen data). Below is a breakdown of how **Bitcoin** and **Monero** are used on the Dark Web:

1. Bitcoin (BTC)

Bitcoin is the most widely used cryptocurrency on the Dark Web due to its **early adoption** and **global recognition**. It operates on a **public ledger** (the blockchain), which records all transactions and makes them **traceable**. While Bitcoin offers a level of pseudonymity (allowing users to create and control addresses without revealing their personal identity), it does not provide complete anonymity.

- **Bitcoin in Dark Web Markets**: Bitcoin is primarily used for **purchasing illicit goods** such as **drugs**, **weapons**, and **stolen credit card information**. Marketplaces on the Dark Web often require payment in Bitcoin to facilitate anonymous exchanges. Bitcoin's wide acceptance on Dark Web platforms like **AlphaBay** and **Silk Road** helped cement its role as the currency of choice for these marketplaces.

- **Bitcoin as a Gateway to Privacy**: Some users employ **Bitcoin mixers** or **tumblers**, which are services that mix Bitcoin transactions from multiple users, making it harder to trace the origin of a transaction. However, using these services still does not guarantee full anonymity.

2. Monero (XMR)

Monero is a privacy-focused cryptocurrency that is gaining popularity on the Dark Web because of its **strong privacy features**. Unlike Bitcoin, Monero transactions are **completely private** and **untraceable**. This is achieved using several cryptographic techniques, such as **Ring Signatures**, **Stealth Addresses**, and **RingCT** (Ring Confidential Transactions).

- **Ring Signatures**: These signatures obscure the identity of the sender by mixing their transaction with those of other users. This makes it nearly impossible to determine which transaction belongs to which sender.

- **Stealth Addresses**: Monero uses **one-time addresses** for each transaction, ensuring that the recipient's address is not revealed in the blockchain. This protects both the recipient and the sender's identity.

- **RingCT**: RingCT ensures that the transaction amount is hidden from the public ledger, adding another layer of privacy.

- **Monero in Dark Web Markets**: Because of its **enhanced privacy**, Monero is often preferred by users engaged in **illicit activities** on the Dark Web. Many **Dark Web marketplaces** that were once dominated by Bitcoin have increasingly adopted Monero as a preferred payment method due to its superior privacy features.

- **Monero for Privacy-Conscious Transactions**: Individuals who want to make secure, private payments for **legal** or **illicit** services use Monero to avoid the potential for their financial transactions to be traced or linked to their identity.

3. Other Cryptocurrencies

While **Bitcoin** and **Monero** dominate Dark Web transactions, other cryptocurrencies like **Ethereum, ZCash**, and **Dash** also play a role. **Ethereum** is commonly used for **smart contracts** and decentralized applications, while **ZCash** uses **zero-knowledge proofs** to enable private transactions. **Dash**, which features **InstantSend** and **PrivateSend**, offers additional privacy features, but is less commonly used than Bitcoin or Monero on the Dark Web.

Real-World Example: The Rise of Bitcoin's Role in Illicit and Legal Dark Web Marketplaces

The rise of **Bitcoin** has had a profound impact on the way the **Dark Web** operates. Bitcoin's pseudonymous nature, combined with its ease of use and decentralized infrastructure, made it the perfect fit for the **illicit marketplaces** that flourished on the Dark Web.

Example 1: The Silk Road

The **Silk Road**, one of the most infamous Dark Web marketplaces, is often cited as the turning point in Bitcoin's adoption on the Dark Web. Launched in 2011 by **Ross Ulbricht** (who operated under the pseudonym **Dread Pirate Roberts**), the Silk Road allowed users to buy and sell **illegal goods** (especially drugs) using Bitcoin.

- **Bitcoin's Role**: Bitcoin was the exclusive payment method on Silk Road, allowing users to transact anonymously and evade traditional financial systems. Silk Road's use of Bitcoin helped establish the cryptocurrency as the go-to currency for Dark Web transactions, as it provided the necessary **pseudonymity** for illicit exchanges.

86

- **Bitcoin's Global Reach**: The Silk Road's success demonstrated how Bitcoin could be used for transactions that spanned the globe, with buyers and sellers from all over the world using the cryptocurrency to facilitate purchases without the need for intermediaries like banks.

- **The Takedown of Silk Road**: In 2013, the FBI seized Silk Road and arrested Ulbricht, but by then, Bitcoin had already established its dominance on the Dark Web. Although Silk Road was shut down, the **legacy of Bitcoin on the Dark Web** lived on, with other marketplaces rising to take its place, continuing to accept Bitcoin as a primary method of payment.

Example 2: Monero's Growing Adoption

As **law enforcement agencies** and security experts grew more adept at tracking Bitcoin transactions, many Dark Web marketplaces and users began to shift to **Monero** due to its **superior privacy features**.

- **Monero's Role**: Platforms like **AlphaBay** (another major Dark Web marketplace) and **Dream Market** embraced Monero alongside Bitcoin, offering users the ability to make truly **anonymous transactions**.

The move towards Monero was fueled by its resistance to **transaction tracing**, which made it more difficult for authorities to track illicit activities on the Dark Web.

- **Monero's Popularity**: The increasing use of Monero can be attributed to the cryptocurrency's ability to offer **true privacy**, which became an essential feature for Dark Web users. While Bitcoin's **traceable** nature made it less ideal for certain types of Dark Web activities, Monero's **untraceability** made it the preferred choice for illegal transactions.

- **Real-World Use**: Many Dark Web vendors now accept both Bitcoin and Monero, and some markets have even **shifted entirely to Monero**, citing the desire to provide better security and privacy for their users.

Conclusion

Cryptocurrencies like **Bitcoin** and **Monero** have fundamentally reshaped the Dark Web by providing a **secure**, **anonymous**, and **decentralized** method of conducting financial transactions. Bitcoin was the first cryptocurrency to gain widespread use on the Dark Web, especially in early illicit marketplaces like **Silk Road**. Its success demonstrated the need for privacy in financial transactions, leading to the adoption of **Monero**, which offers even greater privacy features to users who seek to remain **completely anonymous**.

As cryptocurrencies continue to evolve, so too will their role in the Dark Web. While Bitcoin remains a dominant force, **Monero** and other privacy-focused cryptocurrencies are increasingly becoming the **payment method of choice** for those involved in the more illicit aspects of the Dark Web. For users seeking privacy and security, cryptocurrency remains an essential tool for safeguarding their online activities and transactions.

In the coming chapters, we will explore how cryptocurrencies are used for both **illicit and legal activities** on the Dark Web, how they are integrated into marketplaces and other services, and the legal and ethical considerations surrounding their use.

CHAPTER 9

How to Set Up and Use Tor Safely

A Step-by-Step Guide to Setting Up and Accessing the Dark Web

Tor (The Onion Router) is the most popular and widely used tool to access the **Dark Web** securely. By routing internet traffic through multiple relays and applying layers of encryption, Tor ensures that users remain **anonymous** and **private** while accessing hidden services (such as **.onion** sites). Here's a step-by-step guide to setting up and using Tor to access the Dark Web safely.

1. Download and Install the Tor Browser

The **Tor Browser** is the gateway to the **Dark Web**. It's based on **Mozilla Firefox** and pre-configured to access the Tor network, ensuring your privacy while browsing.

- **Step 1: Download**: Visit the official Tor Project website (https://www.torproject.org) to download the Tor Browser. It's essential to download it only from the official source to avoid counterfeit versions that could contain malware or tracking software.

- **Step 2: Install the Browser**: Once the file is downloaded, follow the installation instructions for your operating system (Windows, macOS, Linux). The installation is straightforward and doesn't require any special configurations.

- **Step 3: Launch the Tor Browser**: After installation, open the Tor Browser. When you launch the browser for the first time, you will be presented with the option to either **connect directly** to the Tor network or use a **bridge** (if you are in a country where Tor is blocked).

2. Configuring and Connecting to the Tor Network

Once the Tor Browser is installed and running, the next step is to connect to the Tor network:

- **Step 1: Connect to Tor**: Click on the **Connect** button when prompted to connect to the Tor network. The browser will automatically configure your connection by selecting the best route through the Tor network's relays.

- **Step 2: Testing the Connection**: After successfully connecting, Tor will ask you if you'd like to **test the connection**. This test ensures that your connection is anonymous, and your internet traffic is being routed through the Tor network.

- **Step 3: Accessing .onion Sites**: You can now access websites with **.onion** domains, which are exclusive to the Tor network. Simply type the **.onion** address of a website into the browser's address bar.

3. Accessing the Dark Web via .onion Sites

After connecting to Tor, you are now ready to start browsing the **Dark Web** and accessing hidden services.

- **Step 1: Find Trusted .onion Sites**: It's important to use only **trusted** and **legitimate** .onion sites. The **Dark Web** is filled with both **legal** and **illicit** content, so proceed cautiously. Trusted directories like **DuckDuckGo** (Dark Web version) or **The Hidden Wiki** can help you find reliable .onion sites.

- **Step 2: Browse the Dark Web Safely**: As you browse, remember that **.onion sites** are designed for anonymity, but your actions can still be traced if you're not careful. Always follow **safety precautions** to ensure your privacy is maintained.

Safety Precautions and Best Practices for New Users

While Tor offers strong **anonymity** and **privacy** features, it's still essential to follow specific **safety precautions** to fully protect your identity and personal information when accessing the Dark Web. Here are some best practices:

1. Don't Use Your Real Identity

- **Avoid personal information**: Never use your real name, address, or any personally identifiable information (PII) on the Dark Web. Create a **pseudonym** for browsing.
- **Separate accounts**: If you need to create accounts on Dark Web websites (such as marketplaces or forums), use an **anonymous email** (preferably a **protonmail** or **tutanota** account) and avoid connecting the account to any personal details.

2. Use a VPN with Tor

- **VPN + Tor**: While Tor provides anonymity, using a **VPN** (Virtual Private Network) in conjunction with Tor adds an additional layer of security. A VPN hides your **IP address** from your ISP and adds an extra layer of encryption to your traffic.

o **VPN Before Tor**: Connect to the VPN before using Tor, so your ISP cannot tell that you're using Tor, which could raise suspicion.

o **Avoid VPN leaks**: Choose a reliable VPN provider that doesn't log your activity and ensures no **DNS leaks** (which could expose your real IP address).

3. Don't Download or Open Files from Unknown Sources

- **Be cautious with downloads**: The Dark Web is home to malicious **files** and **malware**. Never download anything unless you're certain of its legitimacy. Even PDFs and images can contain harmful **exploits** that can compromise your device.

- **Use sandboxing software**: Consider using **virtual machines** or **sandboxing software** when interacting with suspicious files. This isolates the file from your primary system, reducing the risk of infection.

4. Don't Use Your Personal Payment Information

- **Cryptocurrency is preferred**: If you're buying goods or services on the Dark Web, always use **cryptocurrencies** like **Bitcoin** or **Monero** for payment. Do not use credit cards or personal bank accounts, as these can be traced to your identity.

- **Bitcoin Mixing Services**: If you're using Bitcoin, consider using a **Bitcoin mixer** or **tumbler** to obscure your transaction history.

5. Be Aware of Scams

- **Don't trust everything you see**: The Dark Web is filled with scams, from fake marketplaces to phishing schemes. Always exercise caution, especially when dealing with **unknown vendors** or suspicious sites. Check reviews, use escrow services, and avoid paying upfront without receiving the product.

Real-World Example: How a User Safely Accessed a .onion Service for the First Time

Let's take a look at a real-world scenario of how a **new user** accessed a **.onion** service for the first time while maintaining their privacy and security.

Scenario: John, a journalist in a country with oppressive internet restrictions, wants to communicate securely with a source using the Dark Web.

Step 1: Setting Up the Tor Browser

John starts by downloading the **Tor Browser** from the official website, ensuring that he is on the correct, secure URL to avoid counterfeit downloads. After installation, John opens the Tor Browser and connects to the Tor network.

Step 2: Using a VPN for Extra Protection

Before accessing any websites, John connects to a **trusted VPN** to hide his IP address from his Internet Service Provider (ISP) and further obscure his online activities.

Step 3: Navigating to a Secure .onion Website

John is looking to access **SecureDrop**, a **.onion** site used by journalists to communicate with whistleblowers. He finds the correct **.onion** address for SecureDrop through a trusted source and enters it in the Tor browser.

Step 4: Creating an Anonymous Email Account

For communication, John creates an **anonymous email** account on **ProtonMail**, ensuring that it does not link to any of his real-life information. He logs into SecureDrop using this anonymous account.

Step 5: Verifying Security

Before sending any sensitive information, John ensures that SecureDrop's **end-to-end encryption** is active. He double-checks that the website is using **HTTPS** and ensures his VPN is still active to prevent any leaks.

Step 6: Sending the Information

John securely submits the document to the journalist via SecureDrop, knowing that both his identity and the whistleblower's identity are protected by Tor's encryption and anonymity.

Conclusion

Setting up and using Tor is relatively straightforward, but safety on the Dark Web requires diligence and caution. By following **best practices** such as using **pseudonyms**, utilizing a **VPN**, and avoiding downloading suspicious files, users can safely navigate the Dark Web while protecting their identity.

In the real-world example, John was able to access a **.onion service** securely and protect his identity, allowing him to communicate safely with a whistleblower. This shows how Tor can be used effectively for **secure communication** in environments where privacy and anonymity are essential. Whether for **journalism**, **activism**, or personal privacy, Tor offers a crucial tool for accessing the Dark Web safely and securely.

CHAPTER 10

Security Challenges and Threats on the Dark Web

Common Threats on the Dark Web: Scams, Hacking, and Malware

While the **Dark Web** offers a space for anonymity and privacy, it also harbors numerous **security threats** that can put users at risk. Because of the relative **lack of regulation** and **oversight**, the Dark Web has become a haven for malicious actors, including hackers, scammers, and cybercriminals. Here are some of the most common threats that users face on the Dark Web:

1. Scams and Fraudulent Marketplaces

Scams are rampant on the Dark Web, often targeting inexperienced or vulnerable users who are looking to purchase illegal goods or services. These scams take many forms and can result in financial losses or compromised personal information.

- **Fake Marketplaces**: One of the most common scams on the Dark Web involves fraudulent marketplaces that mimic legitimate platforms like

Silk Road or AlphaBay. Users are lured into these fake sites and tricked into paying for goods or services that don't exist. After making a payment in cryptocurrency (which is difficult to trace), the scammer disappears, leaving the victim with nothing.

- **Phishing Scams**: Just like in the regular internet, phishing is also a significant threat on the Dark Web. Scammers may set up fake email accounts or websites to trick users into entering their private information, such as cryptocurrency wallet details or personal identification information.

- **Exit Scams**: In the case of marketplaces, **exit scams** occur when an administrator of a marketplace suddenly closes the site and steals users' funds without delivering any goods or services. These scams are particularly devastating for buyers and sellers who have invested significant amounts of money.

2. Hacking and Data Breaches

The Dark Web is home to hackers and **cybercriminals** who often target vulnerable individuals, businesses, and even governments. The environment of the Dark Web provides anonymity for attackers, making it more difficult for law enforcement to track down perpetrators.

- **Hacked Data**: Many Dark Web markets sell **stolen data**, including credit card numbers, social security numbers, medical records, login credentials, and even corporate databases. This information is typically obtained through **data breaches** or **cyberattacks**.

- **Hacker-for-Hire Services**: On the Dark Web, hackers can offer their services for a fee. These hackers can carry out tasks such as **DDoS (Distributed Denial of Service) attacks**, **data breaches**, or even **identity theft** for clients who wish to target individuals or organizations.

- **Ransomware**: A growing concern on the Dark Web is the sale of **ransomware**. Ransomware is malicious software that locks a user's files or computer system and demands payment (usually in cryptocurrency) for the decryption key. Cybercriminals can buy or rent ransomware programs from Dark Web marketplaces to launch attacks against unsuspecting victims.

3. Malware and Exploits

Malware is one of the most insidious threats on the Dark Web. Malware can infect a user's device, steal sensitive information, and compromise their entire system. Hackers often distribute malware through downloads, phishing links, or compromised websites.

- **Trojan Horses**: These are malicious programs disguised as legitimate software or files. When users download or open these files, the trojan horse silently infects their system, allowing hackers to gain access to sensitive data or control over the device.

- **Keyloggers**: These are pieces of software that record every keystroke made by a user, allowing hackers to steal passwords, login credentials, and sensitive personal information without the victim's knowledge.

- **Exploits and Zero-Day Vulnerabilities**: Exploits target **vulnerabilities** in software or hardware that the developer has not yet patched or discovered. Dark Web hackers often sell **zero-day exploits**, which are vulnerabilities that have not yet been disclosed to the public or fixed by the software maker. These exploits can be used to gain unauthorized access to systems, bypass security measures, or launch attacks.

How to Protect Yourself While Browsing the Dark Web

To navigate the **Dark Web** safely and minimize the risk of encountering threats, users must take several important precautions:

1. Use Strong Encryption and Anonymity Tools

- **Tor + VPN**: While **Tor** is essential for accessing the Dark Web, combining it with a **VPN** (Virtual Private Network) can add an extra layer of protection. A VPN hides your IP address and encrypts your traffic, making it even more difficult for adversaries to trace your activities.
- **Use HTTPS**: Ensure that any site you visit on the Dark Web uses **HTTPS** to encrypt data between your browser and the website. This is particularly important for websites where you will input sensitive information, such as login credentials or payment details.

2. Protect Your Digital Identity

- **Avoid Using Personal Information**: Never use your real name, email address, or any personal identifying information on the Dark Web. If you need to create accounts, always use **pseudonyms** and **disposable email addresses**.

- **Anonymous Payments**: When making purchases on the Dark Web, always use **cryptocurrencies** like **Bitcoin** or **Monero**. These allow you to make anonymous transactions. Avoid using traditional payment methods, such as credit cards or bank transfers, as they can be traced back to you.

3. Be Cautious with Downloads

- **Don't Download Suspicious Files**: Never download files or software from untrusted sources on the Dark Web. These files may contain malware, ransomware, or other malicious software. Even PDFs and seemingly harmless documents can be used to deliver malware.

- **Use Sandboxing or Virtual Machines**: If you absolutely need to download something, consider using a **sandbox** (a virtual environment) or a **virtual**

machine. This ensures that any potential malware is contained within the virtual machine and doesn't affect your primary operating system.

4. Verify the Legitimacy of Websites

- **Check Reviews and Reputation**: Before making a purchase or entering personal information on a Dark Web site, check its reputation. Look for **reviews** and feedback from other users. Avoid websites that have poor feedback or those that look unprofessional or suspicious.

- **Look for Escrow Services**: Many Dark Web marketplaces offer **escrow services** to protect both buyers and sellers. When making transactions, ensure that the marketplace offers escrow, where the payment is held until the buyer receives the goods or services. This helps reduce the risk of scams.

5. Stay Up-to-Date with Security Best Practices

- **Use Antivirus and Anti-Malware Software**: Always have up-to-date antivirus software on your device to help detect and block malicious activity.

105

It's essential to have robust **real-time protection** while navigating the Dark Web.

- **Regularly Update Your Software**: Ensure that your **operating system**, **browser**, and any security tools are up-to-date with the latest patches to protect against new exploits and vulnerabilities.

Real-World Example: The Case of a Dark Web Scam and How It Impacted Users

One notable example of a **Dark Web scam** occurred on the **AlphaBay marketplace**, a major Dark Web platform that was seized by law enforcement in 2017. AlphaBay was one of the largest illegal marketplaces, offering a wide range of illicit goods, from drugs and weapons to hacked data and counterfeit documents.

The Scam:

AlphaBay featured a **vendor scam** where buyers were charged for products but never received them. Many sellers, once they received payment in **Bitcoin**, would close their accounts and disappear, leaving the buyer with no recourse. This type of scam was prevalent because of the **anonymity** offered by Bitcoin, which made it nearly impossible for the buyers to track down the scammers or recover their funds.

- **How It Impacted Users**: The scam caused significant financial losses for users who were duped into paying for goods they never received. Some users were lured into purchasing illicit goods at a discount, only to be swindled after making the payment in cryptocurrency. The lack of **buyer protection** or **refund mechanisms** on many Dark Web platforms meant that victims had little to no recourse.

- **Lessons Learned**: This case highlighted the importance of using **escrow services** on Dark Web marketplaces and thoroughly checking the legitimacy of vendors before making payments. It also demonstrated the risks involved in conducting anonymous transactions, where no one is held accountable for fraudulent activities.

Conclusion

The **Dark Web** offers an environment of **anonymity** and **freedom**, but it also presents significant **security**

107

challenges. From **scams** and **fraudulent marketplaces** to **malware** and **hacking**, users must be vigilant and cautious when navigating this hidden side of the internet.

By following **best practices** such as using **Tor** with a **VPN**, **avoiding suspicious downloads**, and using **cryptocurrencies** for anonymous payments, users can significantly reduce the risk of falling victim to these threats. However, as the **Dark Web** continues to evolve, so too do the tactics of cybercriminals and malicious actors.

The **real-world example** of AlphaBay's scams serves as a stark reminder of the importance of **research, precaution,** and **secure transaction methods** when engaging with the Dark Web. While it remains a valuable resource for privacy and free speech, users must remain aware of the risks and take proactive steps to protect themselves from exploitation.

CHAPTER 11

Illicit Activities on the Dark Web

An Overview of Illegal Activities Commonly Associated with the Dark Web

The **Dark Web** has become infamous for its association with **illegal activities**, but it's important to understand that not all of its users engage in illicit behavior. The anonymity and decentralization offered by the Dark Web, however, have made it a haven for **cybercrime**, **fraud**, **drug trafficking**, **hacking services**, and a variety of **illicit trade**.

The Dark Web's lack of regulation, combined with its encryption and **anonymity features**, creates an environment where illegal activity can flourish with relative ease. While **privacy** and **freedom of speech** are legitimate uses of the Dark Web, the space is equally used by criminals to engage in illicit transactions without the risk of being traced by law enforcement.

Here's an overview of some of the most common **illegal activities** associated with the Dark Web:

1. Drug Trade

One of the most notorious illicit activities on the Dark Web is the **sale and purchase of illegal drugs**. Online marketplaces allow users to buy and sell a variety of controlled substances, ranging from **street drugs** like **cocaine**, **heroin**, and **ecstasy** to **pharmaceuticals** like **opioids** and **prescription medications**.

- **How It Works**: Vendors typically advertise their products on **Dark Web marketplaces** using **pseudonyms** and **cryptocurrencies** (such as **Bitcoin** or **Monero**) to ensure anonymity. After receiving payment, the seller ships the drugs, often using methods to **disguise the shipment** or **hide it within legitimate packages**.

2. Weapons Trafficking

The Dark Web is also a platform for the illegal **sale of weapons**, including firearms, explosives, and even **military-grade equipment**. These weapons are often sold with little regard for **international arms control laws** and often bypass government regulations.

- **How It Works**: Similar to the drug trade, Dark Web sellers of weapons typically use **encrypted** communication and **cryptocurrencies** to protect their identities and transactions. The **anonymity** of the Dark Web allows buyers and sellers to conduct transactions without fear of detection.

3. Stolen Data and Identity Theft

The Dark Web is a major marketplace for **stolen data**, including **credit card numbers**, **social security numbers**, **bank account details**, and even **personal identification information** (PII). Cybercriminals who steal personal data often sell it to other criminals or individuals who wish to commit **identity theft** or **fraud**.

- **How It Works**: **Data breaches** from hacked companies, government databases, or compromised personal accounts are sold in bulk on Dark Web marketplaces. Buyers use this information to create **fake identities**, **make fraudulent purchases**, or even steal **tax returns** or **credit**.

4. Hacking Services

The Dark Web also hosts a wide range of **hacking services**, where cybercriminals offer their expertise for a price. These services include **DDoS (Distributed Denial of Service)** attacks, phishing, ransomware deployment, and website defacement.

- **How It Works**: Hacking services are often offered on a **contractual basis**, where the buyer specifies the target (e.g., a company or government website), and the hacker executes the attack. Some hackers even offer **custom-made malware** or **zero-day exploits** to break into protected systems.

5. Child Exploitation

Unfortunately, the Dark Web also hosts some of the most heinous illegal activities, such as the **sale of child exploitation material** and the distribution of **child pornography**. While this represents a small percentage of Dark Web activities, it is a deeply disturbing aspect that has led to increased law enforcement efforts to shut down offending websites and networks.

- **How It Works**: These sites are often hosted on the Dark Web using **Tor** or **I2P**, and content is shared anonymously between users, making it difficult for authorities to track down the perpetrators. However, global law enforcement agencies are constantly working to identify and apprehend individuals involved in this illegal trade.

6. Fake Identification and Fraudulent Documents

Another common illicit activity on the Dark Web is the creation and sale of **fake IDs** and **fraudulent documents**. These include **counterfeit passports**, **driver's licenses**, **birth certificates**, and **bank statements**.

- **How It Works**: Dark Web vendors provide these counterfeit documents to individuals seeking to commit fraud, evade immigration laws, or hide their identities. These documents are often sold for a premium and are sometimes used for illegal immigration, opening bank accounts, or committing crimes.

Exploring Cybercrime, Hacking, and Other Illicit Trade

The Dark Web's role in fostering **cybercrime** and **hacking activities** is significant. It serves as both a marketplace for stolen goods and services and a hub for individuals looking to carry out **illegal cyber activities**. Here's a closer look at the types of cybercrime that thrive on the Dark Web:

113

1. Ransomware as a Service

One of the most notable aspects of **cybercrime** on the Dark Web is the growing trend of **ransomware-as-a-service**. This model allows individuals with little technical expertise to purchase ransomware tools from skilled hackers and launch attacks against individuals or businesses.

- **How It Works**: Cybercriminals use **ransomware** to encrypt the victim's data and demand payment (often in cryptocurrency) for the decryption key. Some Dark Web forums and marketplaces offer **ransomware-as-a-service** packages, providing **easy-to-use** ransomware tools for aspiring cybercriminals to carry out their attacks.

2. Exploit Kits and Malware

The Dark Web is also home to a wide variety of **exploit kits**—tools that allow attackers to find and take advantage of vulnerabilities in websites or networks. Once an exploit kit is deployed, it can be used to install malware on the victim's computer or network, which could then be used for **data theft, bank fraud**, or even **botnet creation**.

- **How It Works**: Hackers can buy or rent **exploit kits** on Dark Web marketplaces, enabling them to target specific

114

vulnerabilities in popular software or operating systems. These kits often come with **user manuals**, making them accessible to individuals with limited hacking experience.

Real-World Example: The Rise and Fall of Silk Road—What It Tells Us About Dark Web Markets

The **Silk Road** is perhaps the most famous Dark Web marketplace in history. Created in 2011 by **Ross Ulbricht** (operating under the alias **Dread Pirate Roberts**), Silk Road facilitated the anonymous sale of **illegal drugs**, **counterfeit goods**, and other illicit items. Its rise and eventual takedown by law enforcement offer important lessons about the nature of Dark Web markets and the complexities involved in policing them.

The Rise of Silk Road

Silk Road provided a **safe, anonymous** platform for buyers and sellers of illegal goods. By using **Tor** and **Bitcoin**, the marketplace allowed users to conduct transactions without revealing their identities. This allowed the site to flourish for several years, attracting both **drug dealers** and **buyers** who wanted to avoid the scrutiny of law enforcement.

- **Bitcoin as a Payment Method**: One of the primary reasons for Silk Road's success was its use of **Bitcoin** as a payment method. The cryptocurrency provided **anonymity** for both buyers and sellers, making it difficult for law enforcement to track transactions or identify users. Silk Road's reliance on Bitcoin helped it gain a reputation as the primary platform for **illegal transactions** on the Dark Web.

The Takedown of Silk Road

In 2013, Silk Road was shut down by the **FBI**, and **Ross Ulbricht** was arrested and charged with multiple crimes, including **money laundering**, **computer hacking**, and **conspiracy to traffic narcotics**. The takedown of Silk Road marked a major victory for law enforcement, but it also revealed the limitations of policing the Dark Web.

- **The Impact of Silk Road's Shutdown**: Although Silk Road was shut down, its **legacy** continues to influence the Dark Web today. The marketplace's success demonstrated the demand for **anonymous marketplaces** where illegal goods and services could be traded without the risk of detection. Silk Road's closure prompted the emergence of new marketplaces, many of which adopted the same anonymity practices—using **Tor** and **Bitcoin**—to ensure the privacy of transactions.

- **The Rise of Copycat Markets**: Following Silk Road's demise, several **copycat markets** emerged, including **AlphaBay**, **Hansa**, and **Dream Market**, which continued to facilitate the sale of illegal goods. These markets remained active for several years, but law enforcement efforts to seize and shut down these marketplaces continue to this day.

Conclusion

The **Dark Web** remains a hub for a wide range of **illicit activities**, including **drug trafficking**, **weapon sales**, **cybercrime**, and **fraudulent services**. The anonymity and decentralization it provides make it a haven for **criminal enterprises** and individuals seeking to evade law enforcement and traditional financial systems.

While the Dark Web also serves legitimate purposes, such as **protecting privacy** and enabling **free speech**, it is undeniably tied to **illegal markets** and activities. The **rise and fall of Silk Road** exemplifies the dangers of Dark Web marketplaces, and its eventual takedown demonstrated the challenges law enforcement faces in policing this hidden part of the internet.

As the Dark Web continues to evolve, so too do the tactics used by law enforcement to combat illegal activities. The **lesson of Silk Road** is clear: While the Dark Web may offer anonymity, it does not make individuals immune from prosecution, and the illegal activities that thrive within it are never completely secure from law enforcement intervention.

CHAPTER 12

The Dark Web's Underground Markets

Exploring the World of Dark Web Marketplaces

The **Dark Web** is home to a vast number of **underground marketplaces** where users can buy and sell illicit goods and services. These marketplaces operate on **Tor** or **I2P**, using **cryptocurrencies** like **Bitcoin** and **Monero** to enable anonymous transactions. While these markets are often associated with illegal activities, such as **drug trafficking**, **weapon sales**, and **cybercrime**, they also provide access to a range of **legal goods** in certain cases.

Dark Web marketplaces are designed to maintain **anonymity** for both buyers and sellers, allowing users to exchange goods and services without revealing their true identities. These marketplaces typically operate with **pseudonyms**, encrypted communication, and **escrow services** to ensure that transactions are secure and that the buyers receive their purchased items.

1. The Structure of Dark Web Marketplaces

Dark Web marketplaces share some common features, although each marketplace can vary in terms of size, reputation, and product offerings. Here's a breakdown of the key features typically found on these marketplaces:

- **User Accounts**: Just like e-commerce platforms, most Dark Web marketplaces require users to create accounts to browse and make purchases. However, unlike traditional platforms, these accounts do not require personal information like real names or addresses. Instead, users can create pseudonymous accounts and use **anonymous email addresses**.

- **Product Listings**: Sellers post product listings with descriptions, prices, and photos of their goods. The goods offered range from **illegal drugs** and **weapons** to **stolen data**, **fake IDs**, and **counterfeit documents**.

- **Escrow Services**: To protect both buyers and sellers, many marketplaces offer **escrow services**. In an escrow transaction, the buyer's payment is held by the marketplace until the goods are received. If the buyer is satisfied with the product, the payment is released to the seller. If the transaction is disputed, the marketplace steps in to resolve the issue.

- **Cryptocurrency Payments**: **Bitcoin** is the most commonly used cryptocurrency on the Dark Web, although **Monero**, **ZCash**, and other privacy-centric currencies are gaining popularity due to their enhanced anonymity features. These cryptocurrencies allow users to make payments without revealing their identities.

- **Feedback and Ratings**: Similar to platforms like eBay, many Dark Web marketplaces allow buyers to leave feedback and rate sellers based on the quality of their products and services. This system helps create a reputation for sellers and gives buyers some assurance of the reliability and trustworthiness of a seller before making a purchase.

What is Bought and Sold on These Marketplaces?

The range of products and services sold on the Dark Web is vast, and while some are **illegal**, others cater to privacy-conscious individuals or provide legitimate services. Here's an overview of the types of goods and services that are commonly bought and sold on these marketplaces:

1. Illegal Goods

Dark Web marketplaces are often notorious for their involvement in **illegal trade**, providing a platform for cybercriminals, drug dealers, and arms traffickers. Some of the most commonly sold illicit goods include:

- **Drugs**: Illegal substances are perhaps the most commonly traded items on Dark Web marketplaces. Users can buy everything from **street drugs** like **cocaine**, **heroin**, and **ecstasy** to prescription medications like **opioids**, **benzodiazepines**, and **amphetamines**. Some marketplaces even specialize in particular drug types or regions.
- **Weapons**: Firearms, explosives, and other weapons are also commonly traded on the Dark Web. Buyers can purchase everything from handguns and rifles to **military-grade weapons**, **ammunition**, and even **explosive devices**. These transactions often bypass national laws and regulations on weapon ownership.
- **Stolen Data**: Dark Web marketplaces are a hub for the sale of **stolen personal data**, including **credit**

card numbers, social security numbers, medical records, and **bank account information**. These stolen credentials are often used for **identity theft, fraud**, or **money laundering**.

- **Fake IDs and Counterfeit Documents**: Fake **identification cards, passports, driver's licenses**, and **birth certificates** are regularly sold on Dark Web marketplaces. These counterfeit documents are often used for **immigration fraud, money laundering**, and **identity theft**.

- **Malware and Hacking Tools**: Cybercriminals often sell **malware** (such as ransomware, trojans, and keyloggers) on the Dark Web. These tools are designed to infect systems, steal data, or hold files hostage. **Hacking services**, such as **DDoS attacks** or **phishing kits**, are also sold to other cybercriminals looking to exploit vulnerabilities.

2. Legal Goods and Services

While the Dark Web is known for its illegal trade, some marketplaces also cater to individuals who seek **privacy, security**, and **freedom of expression**. These products and services include:

- **Privacy Tools**: Many Dark Web marketplaces sell **VPNs**, **encrypted messaging apps**, and **secure email services**. These tools are often used by individuals in repressive regimes to protect their privacy and evade government surveillance.

- **Whistleblowing Platforms**: There are also marketplaces that provide secure platforms for **whistleblowers** to anonymously share sensitive information with journalists, such as **SecureDrop**. These services are used by individuals looking to expose **government corruption**, **corporate malfeasance**, or **human rights abuses**.

- **Digital Goods**: Some legal products are sold on the Dark Web, including **ebooks**, **software**, and **music**. While many of these items are pirated, some are legitimate digital goods offered by independent sellers who value the anonymity of the Dark Web.

- **Books and Research**: Academic research, books on privacy and digital security, and other educational content can also be found on the Dark Web, typically offered by individuals or organizations focused on privacy rights and security.

Real-World Example: The Operations of AlphaBay Before Its Shutdown

One of the most significant and influential Dark Web marketplaces was **AlphaBay**, which operated from 2014 until its shutdown by law enforcement in 2017. AlphaBay was an illegal marketplace that provided a platform for the sale of drugs, weapons, hacking tools, and stolen data.

The Rise of AlphaBay

AlphaBay quickly became one of the largest and most popular Dark Web marketplaces due to its **wide range of illegal goods** and **user-friendly interface**. It operated similarly to popular e-commerce platforms like **Amazon** or **eBay**, with product listings, user feedback, and escrow services to ensure secure transactions.

- **Marketplace for Illicit Goods**: AlphaBay offered a vast array of **illegal products**, including **drugs, weapons, hacked data, counterfeit documents**, and **malware**. It was also known for its **cybercrime services**, where hackers could offer their skills for hire, from **DDoS attacks** to **identity theft**.

- **Cryptocurrency Payments**: AlphaBay used **Bitcoin** and **Monero** as its primary payment methods, ensuring that transactions could be conducted with **anonymity**. This was a key factor in its success, as both buyers and sellers were drawn to the platform's ability to offer **secure, untraceable transactions**.

- **Global Reach**: AlphaBay attracted users from around the world due to its **multilingual interface** and ability to facilitate international transactions. Buyers could access products from various regions and vendors, while sellers could reach a global customer base.

The Takedown of AlphaBay

In July 2017, AlphaBay was **seized** by law enforcement agencies, including the **FBI**, **Europol**, and other international agencies, in a **global operation**. The marketplace was taken down after the arrest of its creator, **Alexandre Cazes**, who operated under the alias **Alex**. Cazes was found dead in what was ruled as a **suicide** shortly after AlphaBay's seizure.

- **Impact on Users**: The takedown of AlphaBay sent shockwaves through the Dark Web community, as it was one of the largest and most well-established platforms for illegal trade. Many buyers and sellers were left without access to their funds, and countless transactions were disrupted. The incident also served as a warning to other Dark Web marketplace operators that law enforcement was increasingly capable of infiltrating and shutting down illicit operations.

- **The Aftermath**: Following the shutdown of AlphaBay, **numerous copycat markets** emerged, but many were short-lived or shut down by law enforcement. AlphaBay's rise and fall highlighted the **cybercrime economy** on the Dark Web and demonstrated the **vulnerabilities** of these marketplaces to law enforcement actions.

Conclusion

The **Dark Web's underground markets** continue to thrive as hubs for **illicit trade**, including the sale of **drugs**, **weapons**, **stolen data**, and **hacking services**. These markets operate similarly to legitimate e-commerce platforms, offering **anonymous** and **secure transactions** for illegal goods and services. While some markets cater to privacy-conscious users seeking **legal services**, the Dark Web remains primarily known for its **cybercrime economy**.

The rise and fall of **AlphaBay** serve as a stark reminder of the **vulnerabilities** inherent in Dark Web marketplaces. Despite the **anonymity** and **decentralization** that these platforms offer, they are susceptible to law enforcement intervention, and their operators and users are not immune to prosecution. As the Dark Web continues to evolve, its **underground markets** will remain a focal point for illicit trade and cybercrime, though they will also continue to face increasing scrutiny and attempts at shutdown by law enforcement agencies worldwide.

CHAPTER 13

Drugs, Weapons, and Other Illegal Goods

A Closer Look at the Illegal Trade in Drugs, Weapons, and Other Contraband

The **Dark Web** has long been a hotbed for illegal trade, with **drugs**, **weapons**, and other illicit goods often featured prominently on marketplaces. Due to the **anonymity** and **cryptocurrency transactions** provided by platforms like **Tor** and **I2P**, the Dark Web offers a space where sellers and buyers can interact without the typical scrutiny from authorities. However, this doesn't mean the market is immune from law enforcement efforts to combat the **illicit trade**. Here's a closer look at the types of illegal goods most commonly traded on the Dark Web:

1. Drugs

The sale of **illegal drugs** is one of the most prominent activities on the Dark Web. From street drugs like **cocaine**, **heroin**, and **ecstasy** to prescription drugs like **opioids**, **benzodiazepines**, and **stimulants**, the Dark Web marketplaces provide a venue for buyers and sellers to conduct transactions that bypass traditional drug laws.

- **How It Works**: Dark Web drug dealers typically create **listings** for their products on marketplace platforms, offering buyers a wide variety of substances. Payment is usually conducted via **Bitcoin** or other cryptocurrencies, providing anonymity for both the buyer and seller. Once the payment is confirmed, drugs are **disguised** and shipped to the buyer, often using techniques to evade detection by customs or law enforcement agencies.

- **Challenges for Law Enforcement**: The anonymity provided by **Tor** and the use of **cryptocurrencies** make it difficult for authorities to trace the identities of those involved in the drug trade. Furthermore, the sheer volume of transactions and the **decentralized nature** of the Dark Web mean that there are always new markets emerging to replace those taken down by law enforcement.

2. Weapons

The sale of **firearms** and other **weapons** is another major issue on the Dark Web. While these markets are smaller in comparison to the drug trade, they still represent a serious concern, particularly in the context of **international arms trafficking**.

- **How It Works**: Weapons are sold in much the same way as drugs on the Dark Web, with listings that include pictures, descriptions, and prices. Buyers often use **cryptocurrency** for payments, and the weapons are typically shipped using methods designed to avoid detection by law enforcement or customs officials.

- **Challenges for Law Enforcement**: The **anonymity** provided by the Dark Web, combined with the use of **encryption** and **decentralized hosting**, makes it very difficult for law enforcement agencies to trace weapon sales. Additionally, the **international reach** of the Dark Web means that weapons can be traded across borders, making it harder for a single jurisdiction to crack down on the activity.

3. Stolen Data and Hacked Services

The Dark Web is also a marketplace for **stolen data**, including **credit card numbers**, **login credentials**, **medical records**, and **bank account details**. These goods are often sold by hackers who have obtained the information through **data breaches**, **phishing attacks**, or **other illicit means**.

- **How It Works**: Stolen data is often sold in bulk, with hackers offering **credit card numbers**, **social security numbers**, and **personal identifying information** (PII) for a price. These goods are frequently used by cybercriminals for **identity theft**, **fraud**, or to **open fraudulent accounts**.

- **Challenges for Law Enforcement**: Stolen data is often **anonymized** through the use of **cryptocurrency** and **fake identities**, making it difficult for law enforcement to trace the origin of the data or the individuals responsible for the theft. Moreover, the **global nature** of Dark Web markets means that stolen data can be sold across jurisdictions, making international cooperation between law enforcement agencies crucial in combating the trade.

4. Counterfeit Documents

The sale of **fake IDs, passports, driver's licenses**, and other **fraudulent documents** is another significant illicit trade on

132

the Dark Web. These documents are often used by criminals for **identity theft, illegal immigration**, or **financial fraud**.

- **How It Works**: Dark Web vendors offer a variety of fake documents, including high-quality counterfeits that are difficult to distinguish from legitimate IDs. Buyers typically use **cryptocurrency** for payment, and the documents are shipped via the same anonymous methods used for drugs and weapons.
- **Challenges for Law Enforcement**: Counterfeit documents are a serious issue because they can facilitate a wide range of criminal activity, from **immigration fraud** to **money laundering**. The Dark Web makes it easier for individuals to obtain fake documents without being detected, as traditional methods of verification (such as ID checks) are bypassed by the anonymity provided on these platforms.

The Complexities of Policing This Market

While the Dark Web offers significant anonymity, it also presents major challenges for law enforcement agencies. Policing illegal markets on the Dark Web is a complex and multifaceted task that involves not just tracking the illicit transactions themselves but also identifying and apprehending the people behind them. Here are some of the complexities law enforcement faces when trying to combat the illegal trade on the Dark Web:

1. Anonymity and Encryption

The use of **Tor** and **I2P** networks, along with the encryption of communications and transactions, makes it difficult for law enforcement agencies to trace the origins of illegal goods or identify the individuals involved in these activities.

- **Encryption**: Dark Web marketplaces use encryption to secure transactions and communications, ensuring that only the buyer and seller have access to the information. This makes it difficult for law enforcement to intercept communications or identify the parties involved.

- **Cryptocurrency**: Cryptocurrencies like **Bitcoin** and **Monero** are frequently used for transactions on Dark Web markets. While Bitcoin offers a degree of pseudonymity, **Monero** offers even stronger privacy features, making it extremely difficult to trace the flow of funds.

2. Jurisdictional Issues

Since Dark Web marketplaces are accessible from anywhere in the world, the goods and services sold on these platforms often cross national borders. This creates significant **jurisdictional issues** for law enforcement, as authorities in one country may not have the legal authority to investigate crimes committed in another country.

- **International Cooperation**: To combat Dark Web crime, law enforcement agencies from different countries must work together to share information, investigate criminal activity, and take down illegal markets. This requires coordination between organizations like **Europol**, **FBI**, and other national law enforcement bodies.

3. Difficulty in Infiltrating Dark Web Markets

Infiltrating and identifying criminal activity on the Dark Web can be particularly difficult because of the **pseudonymous nature** of the platform and the use of **encrypted communications**. While traditional police work often relies on informants or undercover operations, the **hidden nature** of Dark Web markets makes it hard for law enforcement agents to pose as buyers or sellers without being detected.

- **Undercover Operations**: Although law enforcement agencies have successfully infiltrated some Dark Web markets (such as AlphaBay and Silk Road), these operations require significant expertise, resources, and risk management to carry out successfully.

Real-World Example: How Authorities Shut Down Illegal Dark Web Drug Networks

One of the most high-profile and successful operations against Dark Web drug networks was the **shutdown of Silk Road** in 2013. Silk Road was one of the first and most notorious Dark Web marketplaces, specializing in the sale of illegal drugs, weapons, and other illicit goods. Here's how authorities took down the Silk Road and dismantled its illegal drug network:

The Silk Road Takedown

- **Operation**: The **FBI**, working in cooperation with other international law enforcement agencies, initiated an investigation into the Silk Road marketplace in 2012. The investigation involved **cyber surveillance**, **intelligence gathering**, and the tracking of **Bitcoin transactions** associated with the marketplace.

- **Ross Ulbricht's Arrest**: The creator of Silk Road, **Ross Ulbricht** (operating under the alias **Dread Pirate Roberts**), was arrested in **October 2013** by the FBI at the **San Francisco Public Library**. Ulbricht's arrest marked a significant victory for law enforcement and sent a strong message to other Dark Web marketplace operators.

- **Impact on the Drug Trade**: After Silk Road's closure, a number of other illegal drug marketplaces emerged, such as **AlphaBay** and **Hansa Market**. These marketplaces were also eventually shut down in coordinated law enforcement operations. The takedowns demonstrated the increasing ability of law enforcement to track and dismantle Dark Web drug networks, even when they operated with significant security measures.

- **Lessons Learned**: The Silk Road operation highlighted the role of **cryptocurrency** in facilitating the Dark Web drug trade. Authorities learned how to track Bitcoin transactions to identify the flow of funds between buyers and sellers, leading to the eventual arrest and conviction of Ulbricht.

Conclusion

The **Dark Web's illegal trade** in **drugs, weapons**, and **contraband** remains a significant challenge for law enforcement agencies worldwide. These markets are driven by the **anonymity** offered by platforms like **Tor** and **I2P**, and transactions are secured using **cryptocurrencies**, making it difficult to trace illegal activity. Despite these challenges, **law enforcement** has made significant strides in infiltrating and shutting down Dark Web marketplaces, such as **Silk Road** and **AlphaBay**, through **international cooperation**, **cyber surveillance**, and innovative investigative techniques.

As the Dark Web continues to evolve, it's clear that while **anonymity** and **decentralization** may make it difficult to combat illegal activities, law enforcement agencies are adapting and finding ways to dismantle these criminal networks. However, the **complexity** of policing the Dark Web and the **global nature** of the markets indicate that the fight against Dark Web crime is ongoing and will require continued cooperation, technological innovation, and international coordination.

CHAPTER 14

Hacking, Cybercrime, and the Dark Web

How Cybercriminals Use the Dark Web for Their Activities

The **Dark Web** serves as an ideal environment for **cybercriminals** to operate in relative secrecy and anonymity. Due to the encryption and **pseudonymity** offered by platforms like **Tor** and **I2P**, cybercriminals can engage in a variety of **illegal activities** without easily being traced by law enforcement. The Dark Web is a marketplace for tools, services, and stolen data that facilitate **hacking** and **cybercrime**. Here's an overview of how cybercriminals leverage the Dark Web for illicit activities:

1. Buying and Selling Hacking Tools

One of the most significant ways that cybercriminals use the Dark Web is to **buy and sell hacking tools**. The marketplace is flooded with **malware**, **exploit kits**, and **zero-day vulnerabilities** that enable cybercriminals to launch attacks on individuals, businesses, or governments.

- **Exploit Kits**: Dark Web vendors sell **exploit kits** that target vulnerabilities in popular software or websites. These kits allow even less skilled hackers to **remotely access** systems and **install malware**. Some exploit kits come with **user manuals**, making them accessible to a broader audience of cybercriminals.

- **Ransomware**: Ransomware tools are also available for purchase, enabling individuals to lock down an organization's files and demand payment in exchange for the decryption key. These tools are sold as part of **ransomware-as-a-service** offerings, where individuals can rent or buy pre-built ransomware tools to execute attacks without having to build them from scratch.

- **Malware and Trojan Horses**: The Dark Web is also a hub for the sale of **malicious software** designed to infect systems, steal information, or gain remote access. These programs often come disguised as legitimate software, tricking users into downloading and installing them on their systems.

2. Stolen Data and Identity Theft

Cybercriminals often use the Dark Web to **buy and sell stolen data**. This can range from **credit card information** and **bank account details** to **social security numbers**, **medical records**, and **login credentials**. Cybercriminals use this data for identity theft, financial fraud, and a variety of other illegal activities.

- **Data Breaches**: The Dark Web serves as a marketplace for stolen data obtained through **data breaches**. Cybercriminals often sell vast quantities of stolen data, including usernames, passwords, and other personal information. Once sold, this data can be used to **hack accounts**, **steal money**, or even launch further attacks.

- **Phishing Kits**: The Dark Web also hosts **phishing kits**, which allow cybercriminals to create fake websites that look like legitimate services (e.g., banks or social media platforms) in order to trick users into revealing their credentials. These kits can be used to harvest personal information at scale.

3. Hacking Services for Hire

In addition to buying tools, cybercriminals can also use the Dark Web to **hire hacking services**. Individuals or groups offering their services as professional hackers can be found on these marketplaces, where they are hired to carry out various illegal activities.

- **DDoS Attacks**: Distributed Denial of Service (**DDoS**) attacks are common on the Dark Web, where cybercriminals flood a target's network with traffic, causing it to crash or become unreachable. These attacks can be bought as services, often with specific **targets** in mind.

- **Ransomware Deployment**: Cybercriminals can hire hackers to deploy **ransomware** attacks on specific targets, such as businesses, government agencies, or individuals. This is part of the **ransomware-as-a-service** trend, where the Dark Web acts as a marketplace for these attacks.

The Rise of Ransomware and the Role of the Dark Web in Its Distribution

Ransomware has become one of the most prominent cybercrimes in recent years, and the Dark Web plays a central role in its rise. Ransomware is malicious software that encrypts a victim's data, rendering it inaccessible. The attacker then demands a ransom, usually in **cryptocurrency**, for the decryption key that will unlock the files.

1. How Ransomware Works

Ransomware typically infects systems through a variety of means, including **phishing emails**, **malicious downloads**, and **exploited software vulnerabilities**. Once the ransomware is installed on a victim's system, it **encrypts** files, making them inaccessible to the user. The attacker then demands payment in **cryptocurrency**, promising to provide a decryption key once the ransom is paid.

- **Payment in Cryptocurrency**: Cryptocurrency, particularly **Bitcoin**, is often the preferred payment method for ransomware attacks due to its **pseudonymity** and **difficulty in tracing**. This makes it ideal for cybercriminals who wish to remain anonymous while collecting ransoms.

2. Ransomware-as-a-Service on the Dark Web

The rise of **ransomware-as-a-service** on the Dark Web has made it easier for anyone, even those with little technical expertise, to launch ransomware attacks. These services are marketed on **Dark Web marketplaces** and provide ready-made ransomware tools to criminals looking to extort money from victims.

- **Easy-to-Use Ransomware**: Ransomware-as-a-service platforms allow users to pay for access to pre-made ransomware, which can be easily deployed without having to develop the malware themselves. These services often include **detailed guides** on how to carry out the attack and may even offer **technical support** to ensure successful deployment.

- **The Ransomware Economy**: These services have created a whole ecosystem on the Dark Web, where ransomware creators sell their tools, and hackers who don't have the skills to create the malware themselves can purchase and use these tools. This has **lowered the barrier to entry** for cybercriminals and led to a surge in ransomware attacks.

3. The Victims of Ransomware

Ransomware attacks affect **individuals, businesses**, and **government agencies**. These attacks can cause severe disruption, financial loss, and even damage to reputation, especially for businesses. Victims are often **forced to pay the ransom** to regain access to their data, although there's no guarantee that the attacker will actually provide the decryption key after payment.

- **Impact on Businesses**: Ransomware attacks can be devastating for businesses, especially if they result in prolonged downtime or loss of sensitive data. The healthcare, finance, and energy sectors are particularly vulnerable to ransomware attacks, as their operations rely on sensitive and critical data.

Real-World Example: The Impact of the WannaCry Ransomware Attack and Its Dark Web Connections

One of the most infamous examples of a **ransomware attack** that had global consequences is the **WannaCry** ransomware attack, which took place in May 2017. This attack targeted **hundreds of thousands of computers** across 150 countries, infecting systems in industries ranging from healthcare to telecommunications. It was one of the largest and most disruptive ransomware attacks in history, and its connections to the **Dark Web** provide important insights into the growing role of cybercrime on the Dark Web.

The Attack:

- **How It Spread**: WannaCry exploited a vulnerability in **Microsoft Windows** (known as **EternalBlue**), which had been leaked by the hacking group **Shadow Brokers**. Once the ransomware infected a system, it encrypted files and displayed a ransom note demanding payment in **Bitcoin**.

- **The Ransom Demand**: The ransomware demanded a payment of **$300 in Bitcoin** within three days, or the ransom would increase. If the victim did not pay within seven days, the files would be permanently deleted. The use of Bitcoin allowed the attackers to remain anonymous, making it difficult for authorities to trace the funds.

The Dark Web Connections:

- **Sale of Ransomware Tools**: After the WannaCry attack, it was revealed that the **EternalBlue** exploit, which was used to spread the ransomware, had been leaked and sold on **Dark Web forums**. The exploit had originally been developed by the **U.S. National Security Agency** (NSA) and was stolen by hackers who later sold it to criminal organizations on the Dark Web.

- **WannaCry's Impact**: The WannaCry attack demonstrated how **Dark Web marketplaces** facilitated the sale and distribution of **cyberweapons** and **ransomware tools**. The ransomware's widespread impact showed how easily attackers could deploy sophisticated attacks using tools bought or rented from the Dark Web, even without advanced hacking skills.

- **Law Enforcement Response**: In the aftermath of WannaCry, authorities and cybersecurity experts worked together to track down the individuals behind the attack. However, due to the **anonymity** provided by **cryptocurrencies** and the **Dark Web**, the attackers have yet to be fully identified or arrested. The incident highlighted the challenges law enforcement faces in combating **ransomware** and **cybercrime** on the Dark Web.

Conclusion

The **Dark Web** serves as a haven for **cybercriminals** seeking to **buy tools**, **sell stolen data**, and engage in a variety of **illegal activities**. Ransomware has become one of the most prominent forms of **cybercrime** on the Dark Web, with **ransomware-as-a-service** making it easier than ever for individuals to carry out attacks.

The **WannaCry ransomware attack** serves as a stark example of the damage cybercrime can cause, and it underscores the growing role of the **Dark Web** in enabling such activities. While law enforcement continues to fight against these crimes, the **anonymity** and **decentralized nature** of the Dark Web present significant challenges.

As cybercrime continues to evolve, so too does the role of the Dark Web in facilitating it. With **ransomware** attacks on the rise and **exploit kits** becoming more accessible, law enforcement and cybersecurity experts will need to adapt to the increasingly complex landscape of **Dark Web crime**.

CHAPTER 15

Money Laundering and Financial Fraud

How Financial Fraud and Money Laundering Happen on the Dark Web

The **Dark Web** has become a significant venue for **financial fraud** and **money laundering** due to its **anonymity**, **privacy features**, and **lack of regulation**. Criminals utilize this space to conduct financial crimes, often using **cryptocurrency** to hide the flow of illicit funds. Money laundering and financial fraud on the Dark Web are facilitated by the same factors that make it a popular platform for **illegal goods**: a high degree of **secrecy**, **discretion**, and **difficulty in tracing transactions**.

1. Money Laundering on the Dark Web

Money laundering is the process of making illegally obtained funds appear legitimate. On the Dark Web, criminals engage in money laundering by **converting illicit funds** into a form that can be used in the real economy without raising suspicion.

149

- **Cryptocurrency Usage**: Cryptocurrencies like **Bitcoin**, **Monero**, and **Ethereum** are commonly used for laundering money on the Dark Web due to their **anonymity** and **difficulty in tracing transactions**. Criminals use these digital currencies to transfer illicit funds between multiple wallets, making it hard for authorities to track the source and destination of the money.

- **Mixing and Tumbler Services**: One common technique for laundering money on the Dark Web is the use of **Bitcoin mixing services** or **tumblers**. These services pool together transactions from multiple users and redistribute the funds to different wallets, obscuring the origins of the money. This process makes it difficult to trace the flow of funds back to their original source.

- **Shell Companies and Fronts**: Criminals sometimes create **shell companies** or **front businesses** on the Dark Web to launder money. These entities are set up to receive illicit funds from various sources, which are then mixed with legitimate earnings and withdrawn through **falsified invoices** or **fake transactions**. The **Dark Web** facilitates this process by providing services that help create fake identities and legitimate-looking transactions.

2. Financial Fraud on the Dark Web

Financial fraud on the Dark Web encompasses a wide variety of illegal activities, ranging from **identity theft** to **fraudulent banking activity**. The Dark Web provides the tools and platforms necessary for criminals to perpetrate these crimes on a large scale.

- **Stolen Credit Card Information**: One of the most common types of financial fraud on the Dark Web involves the sale of **stolen credit card data**. Cybercriminals buy and sell **credit card numbers**, **bank account details**, and **PIN codes** on the Dark Web, often obtained through **data breaches** or **hacking**. This data is used to make **fraudulent purchases** or withdraw funds from victims' accounts.

- **Phishing Scams**: Criminals also sell **phishing kits** on the Dark Web, which allow users to create **fake websites** that mimic legitimate ones (e.g., banks or online retailers). These fake sites are used to trick

151

individuals into entering their **login credentials** and **financial details**, which are then used for fraud.

- **Fake Investment Schemes**: The Dark Web is also home to fraudulent investment opportunities, including **fake cryptocurrency schemes**, **Ponzi schemes**, and **investment fraud**. Criminals often create websites that promise large returns on investments in digital currencies or other assets, but in reality, these schemes are designed to steal money from unsuspecting investors.

Techniques Used to Cover Up Financial Crimes

To successfully conduct money laundering or financial fraud on the Dark Web, criminals use various techniques to **cover their tracks** and **obfuscate** the origin of the illicit funds. These methods ensure that **law enforcement agencies** and **financial institutions** have difficulty identifying and halting the transactions.

1. Layering

Layering is a technique used to make it difficult to trace the origin of the illicit funds. It involves moving money through a series of transactions designed to obscure the trail. Here's how layering works on the Dark Web:

- **Bitcoin Tumblers**: As mentioned earlier, criminals use **mixing services** or **tumblers** to obfuscate the source of illicit funds. These services shuffle the transactions of multiple users and redistribute the coins to different wallets, making it hard for investigators to track the transactions to their original source.

- **Multiple Wallets**: Criminals will often transfer funds through multiple **wallets**—sometimes hundreds or even thousands of different wallets—before reaching the destination. Each transfer makes it harder to trace the origin of the funds and allows the criminals to spread their transactions across multiple addresses.

- **International Transfers**: Another technique criminals use is transferring funds internationally, often to countries with **weak financial regulations** or where cryptocurrency use is common. These international transfers can make it harder for law enforcement to trace the flow of funds.

2. Integration

Once the illicit funds have been successfully laundered through multiple layers, the final step is **integration**, where the funds are introduced into the legitimate economy.

- **Purchasing Goods**: One way to integrate laundered money is by purchasing **high-value items** on the Dark Web (e.g., **luxury goods**, **electronics**, or **jewelry**). These goods are often resold through legitimate channels to generate clean money that can be deposited into bank accounts.

- **Investment in Legal Businesses**: Some criminals use their laundered funds to invest in **legitimate businesses**, particularly in industries like **cryptocurrency exchanges**, **real estate**, or **online services**. By introducing illicit funds into these businesses, criminals can make it appear as though the money is derived from legitimate sources.

- **Digital Asset Transactions**: With the rise of digital currencies, criminals have begun using **cryptocurrency exchanges** on the Dark Web to exchange illicit funds for legitimate digital assets, which can then be traded or sold on legal platforms.

Real-World Example: The Role of Dark Web Marketplaces in Laundering Money

One of the best-known examples of money laundering on the Dark Web involves the operations of the **Silk Road**, a **Dark Web marketplace** that was shut down by law enforcement in 2013. Silk Road allowed users to buy and sell **illegal drugs**, **weapons**, and **counterfeit documents**, but it also played a central role in **money laundering**.

The Silk Road and Money Laundering

Silk Road facilitated large-scale financial crimes by providing a **platform** where **illicit goods** were exchanged for **cryptocurrency**. Here's how the laundering process worked on the Silk Road:

- **Bitcoin as Payment**: Silk Road exclusively used **Bitcoin** for transactions, enabling users to remain **anonymous** and avoid detection by law enforcement. The use of Bitcoin allowed criminals to make transactions without revealing their identities or the source of the funds.

- **Bitcoin Mixing Services**: Many users of Silk Road employed **Bitcoin tumblers** to launder the funds they earned from illegal transactions. These services helped criminals conceal the origin of their funds, making it nearly impossible for investigators to trace the transactions back to illicit activities.

- **International Transactions**: Silk Road vendors were able to move funds internationally with relative ease, selling drugs and other illegal goods to buyers around the world. The global reach of Silk Road's transactions made it even harder for authorities to track illicit profits.

The Takedown of Silk Road

In October 2013, Silk Road was shut down by the **FBI**, and its creator, **Ross Ulbricht** (alias **Dread Pirate Roberts**), was arrested and charged with various crimes, including **money laundering** and **drug trafficking**. The authorities seized **approximately $28 million in Bitcoin**, a testament to the scale of the illicit transactions that took place on Silk Road.

- **Money Laundering Exposure**: During the investigation, it was revealed that Ulbricht had employed various techniques to launder the funds generated from Silk Road, including the use of Bitcoin mixing services and international Bitcoin transfers. This case highlighted how Dark Web marketplaces can be used to facilitate not only illegal trade but also complex money laundering schemes.

- **Impact on Dark Web Marketplaces**: After Silk Road was taken down, a number of other **Dark Web marketplaces** (such as AlphaBay and Dream Market) continued to operate, but with increased attention from law enforcement agencies. Authorities began to track **cryptocurrency transactions** more rigorously, leading to the shutdown of additional platforms and the arrests of their operators.

Conclusion

The **Dark Web** remains a powerful tool for **money laundering** and **financial fraud** due to its **anonymity**, **decentralized structure**, and reliance on **cryptocurrencies** for transactions. Criminals use the Dark Web to **buy and sell illicit goods**, **launder stolen funds**, and cover up their

157

illegal activities through techniques like **Bitcoin tumbling,
shell companies**, and **international transactions**.

Real-world examples, such as the **Silk Road** takedown,
illustrate how **Dark Web marketplaces** can be used as
platforms for laundering money on a large scale. These cases
also show the challenges law enforcement faces in
combating financial crimes on the Dark Web, particularly
due to the **anonymity** offered by cryptocurrencies and the
complexity of the laundering process.

As law enforcement agencies continue to enhance their
ability to track cryptocurrency transactions and infiltrate
Dark Web markets, it is clear that the fight against **financial
fraud** and **money laundering** on the Dark Web will remain
a top priority. However, the evolving nature of
cryptocurrency and its widespread use means that law
enforcement will need to adapt continually to stay ahead of
these criminal activities.

CHAPTER 16

Privacy and Freedom of Expression on the Dark Web

How the Dark Web Serves as a Tool for Privacy and Free Speech

While the **Dark Web** is often associated with illegal activities, it also plays a critical role in **protecting privacy** and **enabling freedom of expression**. For individuals living under **repressive regimes**, in **high-risk professions**, or in countries with **limited freedom of speech**, the Dark Web offers a **secure, anonymous** space to communicate, share information, and engage in activities without fear of surveillance or persecution.

1. The Role of the Dark Web in Protecting Privacy

In today's world, where personal data is often collected, analyzed, and sold, maintaining **privacy** has become increasingly difficult. The **Dark Web** offers tools and technologies that protect the **privacy** of individuals who want to avoid surveillance and ensure their **personal freedom** is not compromised.

- **Anonymity through Tor and I2P**: The **Tor network** and **I2P** (Invisible Internet Project) are two major tools used on the Dark Web to protect users' identities. These networks route internet traffic through multiple layers of **encryption**, hiding the **IP address** and **location** of users. This **pseudonymity** allows individuals to browse, communicate, and interact online without revealing their personal details or location.

- **Cryptocurrencies for Financial Privacy**: Cryptocurrencies, such as **Bitcoin** and **Monero**, are often used on the Dark Web to facilitate **anonymous transactions**. These digital currencies enable users to make payments and conduct business without exposing their **financial information**, making it difficult for authorities or third parties to track the flow of funds.

2. Enabling Freedom of Expression

In some countries, **freedom of speech** is heavily restricted, and individuals who express dissenting opinions or criticize the government face **surveillance**, **harassment**, or **imprisonment**. The Dark Web provides a platform where these individuals can speak freely, share information, and organize politically without the risk of being censored or persecuted.

- **Access to Censored Information**: In countries with stringent internet censorship laws, the Dark Web acts as a **safe haven** for individuals to access uncensored news, social media platforms, and government documents. People in **China**, **Iran**, and other authoritarian states use the Dark Web to **circumvent censorship** and access the free flow of information.
- **Whistleblowing**: The Dark Web enables whistleblowers to leak information securely, ensuring that their identities remain protected while exposing corruption or wrongdoing. This serves as a vital tool in holding **governments** and **corporations** accountable for unethical or illegal activities.

Examples of Legal and Ethical Uses of the Dark Web

While the Dark Web is often viewed negatively due to its association with illicit activities, it has also been used for **legal** and **ethical** purposes. Many users turn to the Dark Web for **privacy**, **security**, and **freedom of expression** in ways that align with their **fundamental rights**.

161

1. Political Activism and Journalism

For **journalists** and **activists** in oppressive regimes, the Dark Web offers a platform to **share information**, **organize protests**, and **coordinate political activities** without fear of government surveillance or reprisal.

- **Secure Communication**: The Dark Web provides tools that allow journalists and activists to communicate securely, using **encrypted messaging** and **anonymous browsing** to share information without risking their safety. Platforms like **SecureDrop** and **ProtonMail** are frequently used to send confidential information from sources to journalists while maintaining anonymity.

- **Protection from Surveillance**: In countries where activists and journalists face censorship or persecution for their work, the Dark Web offers a safe space to organize, report, and share **sensitive** information. For example, activists in **Syria** and **Hong Kong** have used the Dark Web to bypass government restrictions and communicate without being traced.

2. Whistleblowing and Accountability

The Dark Web serves as an essential tool for **whistleblowers** who wish to expose corruption, government malfeasance, or corporate misconduct without fearing retaliation.

- **SecureDrop**: **SecureDrop** is a platform used by **journalists** and **whistleblowers** to safely communicate and submit documents on the Dark Web. The system uses **end-to-end encryption** to ensure that the identity of the whistleblower remains anonymous, allowing them to leak sensitive information without exposing themselves to danger.

- **Edward Snowden and WikiLeaks**: Perhaps the most famous whistleblower in recent history is **Edward Snowden**, who used tools like Tor to communicate securely with journalists while leaking classified documents about government surveillance programs. Similarly, organizations like **WikiLeaks** have provided a platform for whistleblowers to release confidential government and corporate data, such as **the Iraq War Logs** and **the Panama Papers**.

3. Protection of Privacy for Vulnerable Groups

The Dark Web is also crucial for individuals in vulnerable situations who need to maintain **privacy** and **security**. This includes those who are **victims of domestic violence**, **minorities** at risk of persecution, or individuals **seeking asylum** in countries where their personal safety is at risk.

- **Domestic Violence Survivors**: Victims of **domestic violence** can use the Dark Web to communicate with **support organizations**, access **legal resources**, and seek **shelter** while remaining **anonymous**. They can also use encrypted messaging services to reach out to people who can help them, without their abuser being able to trace their activities.

- **LGBTQ+ Communities in Repressive Countries**: In countries where LGBTQ+ individuals face criminalization or violence, the Dark Web provides a platform where they can **seek information, find safe spaces**, and **connect with support groups** without fear of persecution.

Real-World Example: How Whistleblowers Use the Dark Web to Leak Information Safely

One of the most compelling examples of the **ethical** use of the Dark Web is its role in **whistleblowing**. The Dark Web provides whistleblowers with a secure and anonymous way to **leak sensitive information** without revealing their identity. Below is a real-world example that illustrates how whistleblowers have used the Dark Web to leak information safely:

Example 1: Edward Snowden and the NSA Leaks

In 2013, **Edward Snowden**, a former National Security Agency (NSA) contractor, exposed classified information regarding the United States government's mass surveillance programs. Snowden utilized **Tor** and **encrypted communications** to securely communicate with journalists from **The Guardian** and **The Washington Post**.

- **The Role of the Dark Web**: Snowden used the **Dark Web** to protect his identity while contacting journalists. Through the use of **encrypted messaging** and **secure file-sharing platforms** like

SecureDrop, he was able to safely leak documents without the risk of being traced.

- **The Impact**: Snowden's whistleblowing led to global debates about the balance between **national security** and **individual privacy**. The leaked documents revealed the extent of government surveillance on its citizens, sparking legislative and public discourse around privacy rights and government overreach.

Example 2: The Panama Papers

Another prominent example of whistleblowing that involved the Dark Web is the release of the **Panama Papers** in 2016. The Panama Papers consisted of 11.5 million documents that exposed the offshore financial dealings of politicians, business leaders, and celebrities.

- **The Role of the Dark Web**: The documents were initially shared with **journalists** through **SecureDrop**, an encrypted platform on the Dark Web, ensuring that the sources behind the leaks remained anonymous. The documents revealed how wealthy individuals used offshore accounts to evade taxes and hide assets, leading to significant political and financial ramifications.

- **Global Consequences**: The leak of the Panama Papers led to investigations and the resignation of high-profile figures, including the Prime Minister of Iceland. It also sparked a global conversation about the ethics of offshore tax havens and financial transparency.

Conclusion

While the **Dark Web** is often associated with illegal activities, it also serves as a critical platform for **privacy protection**, **freedom of expression**, and **whistleblowing**. For individuals living under repressive regimes, **journalists**, **activists**, and **vulnerable communities**, the Dark Web offers a space where they can **speak freely**, **share information**, and **protect their identities** without fear of persecution or surveillance.

The **ethical** uses of the Dark Web—such as **whistleblowing** and **secure communication** for activists—demonstrate its importance as a tool for **freedom**, **privacy**, and **accountability**. Real-world examples, like the **Edward**

Snowden leaks and the **Panama Papers**, show the power of the Dark Web in facilitating the safe and anonymous flow of information that holds powerful institutions accountable.

As governments and law enforcement agencies continue to combat **illegal activity** on the Dark Web, it's essential to recognize its positive potential as a platform for **protecting civil liberties**, **preserving privacy**, and enabling **free speech** in a connected world where anonymity and privacy are increasingly at risk.

CHAPTER 17

Law Enforcement and the Dark Web

The Challenge of Policing the Dark Web

Policing the **Dark Web** presents significant challenges for law enforcement agencies due to its **anonymity**, **decentralization**, and **cryptocurrency** use. The Dark Web provides a space where criminals can engage in illegal activities, such as **drug trafficking**, **weapons sales**, **hacking**, and **money laundering**, while avoiding detection by traditional surveillance methods. Law enforcement agencies face a variety of **obstacles** when attempting to monitor and shut down illegal activities on the Dark Web.

1. Anonymity and Encryption

One of the primary challenges in policing the Dark Web is the **anonymity** provided by tools like **Tor** and **I2P**, which obscure the identity and location of users. These networks allow individuals to communicate, browse, and transact anonymously, making it difficult for authorities to trace the users behind illegal activities.

- **Tor Network**: Tor encrypts internet traffic and routes it through a series of **relays**, making it difficult to trace users' **IP addresses** or determine their physical location. This encryption provides a high degree of **privacy**, allowing criminals to carry out illicit activities without revealing their identities.

- **I2P**: Similarly, **I2P** is another anonymous network used on the Dark Web, which makes it difficult for authorities to track traffic or identify users. Unlike Tor, I2P is primarily used for **internal, peer-to-peer communication** within the network, which means it is often employed by cybercriminals to share illegal content or coordinate activities securely.

2. Use of Cryptocurrency

The **use of cryptocurrencies**, such as **Bitcoin** and **Monero**, adds another layer of complexity to policing the Dark Web. Cryptocurrencies allow users to conduct transactions without revealing their identities or relying on traditional financial institutions, making it difficult for law enforcement to trace funds or track illicit transactions.

- **Bitcoin**: While Bitcoin offers a degree of **pseudonymity**, it is still possible to trace transactions to some extent, especially when the cryptocurrency is used in combination with other tools, such as **mixers** or **tumblers**, which further obfuscate the source of funds.

- **Monero**: **Monero** offers even greater privacy than Bitcoin, as it uses **ring signatures** and **stealth addresses** to hide the sender, receiver, and transaction amount. Monero has become the cryptocurrency of choice for criminals who want to conduct transactions without leaving a trace.

3. Decentralization and Lack of Regulation

The **decentralized nature** of the Dark Web means that there is no central authority overseeing its activities. This makes it difficult for law enforcement to target specific actors or marketplaces, as criminals can quickly move to new platforms if their current marketplace or operation is shut down. The lack of regulation on the Dark Web means that **illegal activities** can thrive without the oversight and control typically seen in the physical world.

- **Global Jurisdictional Issues**: The Dark Web is accessible from anywhere in the world, making it a **global** platform. This presents jurisdictional challenges, as law enforcement agencies from different countries must cooperate to investigate and shut down illegal activities. This international cooperation can be hindered by **differing laws** and **regulations** governing online activity in different jurisdictions.

How Authorities Track and Shut Down Illegal Activities on the Dark Web

Despite the challenges, law enforcement agencies have made significant strides in tracking and shutting down illegal activities on the Dark Web. Authorities employ a combination of **cyber surveillance**, **intelligence gathering**, **undercover operations**, and **international cooperation** to target and dismantle criminal operations.

1. Cyber Surveillance and Intelligence Gathering

Law enforcement agencies have developed specialized tools and techniques to monitor **Dark Web marketplaces** and **illicit activities**. These tools allow authorities to gather intelligence and track illegal transactions without directly engaging with the criminal networks.

- **Monitoring Marketplaces**: Law enforcement agencies often monitor Dark Web marketplaces and forums where illegal goods and services are advertised. By tracking user activity and identifying key players in these markets, authorities can gain valuable insights into criminal operations.

- **Data Analysis**: Authorities use **data analysis** techniques to trace cryptocurrency transactions and identify patterns that can lead to the identification of criminal activity. This can involve **blockchain analysis**, which helps track the flow of funds on the Bitcoin blockchain, or examining **transaction metadata** to identify links between buyers, sellers, and criminal organizations.

2. Undercover Operations

In some cases, law enforcement agencies conduct **undercover operations** on the Dark Web to infiltrate illegal marketplaces and gather evidence of criminal activity. These operations involve law enforcement agents posing as buyers, sellers, or administrators to identify criminal activities and collect information that can lead to arrests and prosecutions.

- **Sting Operations**: Law enforcement agencies may set up **sting operations** in which they act as buyers or sellers on illicit marketplaces. By participating in transactions and communicating with criminals, authorities can collect evidence and identify suspects.

- **Vendor Disruption**: Authorities may also infiltrate criminal organizations or online communities on the Dark Web to disrupt illegal activities. For example, law enforcement agents may pose as drug dealers or hackers to gather intelligence and ultimately **shut down** criminal operations.

3. Collaboration and International Cooperation

Because of the global nature of the Dark Web, effective law enforcement requires **international collaboration**. Agencies from different countries must work together to investigate, track, and dismantle criminal networks operating on the Dark Web.

- **Europol and FBI Cooperation**: Agencies like **Europol** and the **FBI** frequently collaborate on investigations involving the Dark Web. These agencies work together to share intelligence, execute joint operations, and take down Dark Web marketplaces and criminal organizations that span multiple countries.

- **Extradition and International Arrests**: In cases where Dark Web criminals are identified, law enforcement agencies may need to work with international counterparts to execute **extraditions** and make arrests. This is especially difficult when the criminals operate from countries with weak enforcement of cybercrime laws.

Real-World Example: The Takedown of Silk Road and Its Impact on Dark Web Security

The **Silk Road** takedown in 2013 was one of the most significant law enforcement actions against a Dark Web marketplace, and it had a profound impact on the security of Dark Web marketplaces and the broader criminal ecosystem.

The Silk Road: A Dark Web Marketplace for Illicit Goods

Silk Road was one of the **largest and most notorious** Dark Web marketplaces, where users could buy and sell illegal goods such as **drugs**, **weapons**, and **counterfeit documents**.

The site was created by **Ross Ulbricht**, who operated under the pseudonym **Dread Pirate Roberts**, and used **Bitcoin** as its primary form of payment. Silk Road's use of **Tor** and **cryptocurrency** made it difficult for authorities to trace transactions or identify users, and it became a hub for illicit trade.

- **The Role of Bitcoin**: Bitcoin's pseudonymous nature was central to Silk Road's operations, as it allowed users to engage in transactions without revealing their identity or location. The use of Bitcoin also made it harder for law enforcement to track and seize illicit funds.

- **The Silk Road Ecosystem**: Silk Road was more than just a marketplace—it was an entire ecosystem that included **vendors**, **buyers**, and **escrow services** that allowed for secure transactions. This created a **self-sustaining criminal enterprise** that operated outside the bounds of the law.

The Takedown of Silk Road

In October 2013, the **FBI** and other law enforcement agencies successfully shut down the Silk Road marketplace and arrested its creator, **Ross Ulbricht**, who was charged with a range of crimes, including **money laundering**, **drug trafficking**, and **computer hacking**. The takedown was the result of an extensive **cyber investigation** that involved **undercover operations**, **intelligence gathering**, and **blockchain analysis**.

- **Operation Disruption**: The Silk Road takedown demonstrated how law enforcement agencies could infiltrate and disrupt Dark Web marketplaces. Investigators used a combination of **cyber surveillance**, **tracing Bitcoin transactions**, and **tracking Ulbricht's digital footprint** to identify him and gather evidence.

- **Seizing Assets**: The authorities seized **approximately 144,000 Bitcoins** from Silk Road's operation, a significant amount of cryptocurrency that was valued at **$28 million** at the time. This seizure highlighted the ability of law enforcement to track and seize cryptocurrency involved in criminal activity.

Impact on Dark Web Security

The Silk Road takedown had a profound effect on Dark Web marketplaces and criminal networks:

177

- **Increased Law Enforcement Focus**: The takedown of Silk Road signaled to other Dark Web marketplaces that law enforcement was becoming more capable of infiltrating and dismantling illegal operations. After the Silk Road's shutdown, other major Dark Web marketplaces, such as **AlphaBay** and **Hansa**, were also taken down by law enforcement.

- **Shift to More Secure Platforms**: In response to the takedown of Silk Road and the increased scrutiny of Dark Web activities, some criminal organizations moved to more **secure and decentralized** platforms, including **I2P** and **private forums** that offered **stronger encryption** and **more anonymity**.

- **Heightened Security Measures**: Following the takedown of Silk Road, Dark Web marketplaces began implementing stronger security measures, such as **more robust encryption**, **multi-signature wallets**, and **additional anti-fraud protocols** to prevent law enforcement infiltration.

Conclusion

The **Dark Web** presents significant challenges for law enforcement due to its **anonymity**, **decentralization**, and **cryptocurrency** use. However, authorities have become increasingly adept at tracking and dismantling **illegal activities** on the Dark Web using **cyber surveillance**, **undercover operations**, and **international cooperation**. The **Silk Road takedown** marked a significant milestone in the battle against Dark Web crime and demonstrated that even the most sophisticated criminal operations can be infiltrated and shut down by law enforcement.

Despite the challenges, law enforcement continues to adapt and develop new techniques to combat Dark Web crime. The **Silk Road** takedown, along with the subsequent shutdowns of **AlphaBay** and **Hansa**, illustrates the increasing effectiveness of global law enforcement efforts to combat **cybercrime** and **illicit trade** on the Dark Web. As the Dark Web evolves, so too will the tactics used by authorities to maintain **security** and **rule of law** in this hidden part of the internet.

CHAPTER 18

The Ethics of Anonymity

An Ethical Discussion of Anonymity Online

Anonymity on the internet, particularly on platforms like the **Dark Web**, has been a subject of intense debate. The ability to **remain anonymous** online provides significant **advantages** in terms of **privacy**, **freedom of expression**, and **security**. However, it also carries inherent **ethical dilemmas**. The central ethical question revolves around whether anonymity should be protected as a basic right or whether it enables and shields harmful actions.

1. The Right to Privacy vs. Accountability

One of the most fundamental ethical arguments surrounding anonymity is the balance between the **right to privacy** and the need for **accountability**. On the one hand, privacy is considered a **fundamental human right**, protecting individuals from unwanted surveillance, profiling, and data collection. On the other hand, complete anonymity can enable **harmful behavior**, such as **cyberbullying**, **fraud**, and **illegal trade**, without any consequence or identification of the wrongdoers.

180

- **Privacy as a Human Right**: Proponents of online anonymity argue that privacy is essential for **freedom of speech**, **personal autonomy**, and **democracy**. Without privacy, individuals may self-censor or avoid expressing dissenting opinions out of fear of being targeted or surveilled by authorities or private entities. In a world where personal data is constantly collected and exploited, **online anonymity** is viewed as a safeguard for personal freedom and autonomy.

- **Accountability and Protection from Abuse**: Opponents of excessive anonymity argue that it allows individuals to hide behind false identities and engage in illegal or unethical behavior without facing any consequences. Anonymity, in this view, becomes a **shield** for cybercriminals, fraudsters, and perpetrators of online abuse. In the case of the **Dark Web**, where illegal activities such as **drug trafficking**, **money laundering**, and **cybercrime** thrive, anonymity can be seen as a facilitator of harm rather than a protector of rights.

2. Ethical Implications of Anonymity on the Dark Web

The Dark Web is an extreme case where anonymity is both an **essential tool** for individuals seeking **privacy** and **freedom of expression** and a **mechanism** for **illicit behavior**. The **ethical** debate surrounding anonymity on the Dark Web involves the question of whether the positive aspects of anonymity outweigh its negative consequences.

- **Freedom of Expression**: For individuals living under **authoritarian regimes**, the Dark Web provides a platform where they can express dissent, share information, and access uncensored content. In these regions, anonymity is not only a tool for **freedom of expression** but also a **matter of survival**. It allows political dissidents, journalists, and activists to challenge oppressive governments without fear of retaliation.

- **Enabling Illicit Activities**: Conversely, anonymity on the Dark Web also facilitates a range of **criminal activities**, including the sale of illegal drugs, weapons, and stolen data. This raises ethical concerns about whether **protecting anonymity** on the Dark Web inadvertently supports criminal behavior that harms society.

The key ethical dilemma, therefore, is whether anonymity should be supported in all cases, given the risks it may pose to **society** and **law enforcement**. Should anonymity be protected as an absolute right, or should it be restricted when it enables harmful activities?

The Benefits and Dangers of Being Anonymous

Anonymity online offers a range of **benefits**, but it also comes with its share of **dangers**. Understanding both sides of this issue is essential to navigating the ethical complexities of online anonymity.

1. The Benefits of Anonymity

- **Protection from Surveillance**: Anonymity allows individuals to protect themselves from **surveillance** by both governments and private corporations. In an age where online activity is often tracked and used for commercial purposes, anonymity offers a layer of **protection** against **data mining**, **targeted advertising**, and **profiling**.
- **Freedom of Expression**: Anonymity can empower individuals to speak freely without fear of

retaliation. In countries where **freedom of speech** is restricted, anonymity enables people to share their opinions, challenge authority, and participate in **political discourse** without fear of being jailed, persecuted, or silenced.

- **Safety for Vulnerable Groups**: Anonymity can be essential for **vulnerable individuals**, including victims of **domestic violence**, **whistleblowers**, and those in **dangerous professions**. For example, individuals fleeing abusive relationships can seek help anonymously without revealing their location to their abuser. Whistleblowers can leak sensitive information securely without fear of retribution. This is particularly important for journalists, activists, and human rights defenders working in dangerous regions.

2. The Dangers of Anonymity

While anonymity offers numerous benefits, it also carries certain **dangers**:

- **Enabling Cybercrime**: Anonymity enables individuals to engage in **illicit activities** without fear of detection. On the Dark Web, this includes **drug**

trafficking, **money laundering**, **child exploitation**, and **hacking**. The lack of accountability can embolden criminals and allow them to exploit anonymity for personal gain.

- **Cyberbullying and Harassment**: Anonymity can be used to harass or harm others online, particularly in the form of **cyberbullying**, **defamation**, and **identity theft**. The ability to hide behind a fake identity or pseudonym allows individuals to target others without the fear of being caught or held accountable for their actions.

- **Lack of Responsibility**: Anonymity can diminish individuals' sense of **responsibility** and accountability. When people feel they can act without being identified, they may engage in harmful behavior that they would not engage in otherwise. This can lead to an increase in **toxic online communities** or the spread of harmful content without fear of consequences.

Real-World Example: How Anonymity Can Protect Journalists and Activists in Dangerous Regions

One of the most powerful and ethical uses of anonymity is for **journalists** and **activists** in **dangerous regions**. In countries with **restrictive regimes**, where freedom of speech and the press is often censored or punished, anonymity provides a way for these individuals to **safely communicate** and share information without putting themselves in jeopardy.

Example 1: The Role of Anonymity in the Arab Spring

During the **Arab Spring** uprisings in 2010–2011, **activists** in countries like **Tunisia**, **Egypt**, and **Syria** used tools like **Tor** and other encrypted communications to organize protests, share information, and communicate with international journalists and human rights organizations. The oppressive regimes in these countries often monitored online activities and suppressed dissident voices, but the use of **anonymity** allowed these activists to evade detection.

- **Tor for Anonymity**: Activists used **Tor** to access social media platforms, post content, and organize events, all while **concealing their identities**. This allowed them to **bypass government censorship** and express their opinions freely, despite the risks involved.

- **Protection for Whistleblowers**: Journalists also used encrypted platforms to receive anonymous tips from whistleblowers within the government or military, providing them with information that would have been otherwise inaccessible. The **anonymity** of these tools ensured that whistleblowers could expose corruption or human rights abuses without fear of imprisonment or retaliation.

Example 2: Anonymity in Journalism

A more recent example is the use of **SecureDrop**, an encrypted platform for whistleblowers and journalists. **The Guardian**, **The Washington Post**, and other major news outlets use SecureDrop to securely receive and publish leaked documents from whistleblowers. This system allows journalists to maintain a safe distance from sources, ensuring that their **identity** remains protected.

- **Edward Snowden** famously used SecureDrop to leak the **NSA surveillance** documents to journalists, which eventually led to global revelations about government surveillance programs. Snowden's use of **Tor** and other anonymity tools allowed him to communicate safely with the media while ensuring that his **identity** and **location** remained concealed.

- **Protection of Sources**: Journalists who cover sensitive topics, such as **corruption**, **political oppression**, and **human rights abuses**, rely on anonymity to protect their sources and preserve the integrity of their reporting. In regions where **journalists** face threats of violence, kidnapping, or imprisonment, the ability to communicate anonymously allows them to continue their work without endangering themselves or their sources.

Conclusion

The **ethics of anonymity** is a complex and nuanced issue, particularly in the context of the **Dark Web**. While anonymity can be a powerful tool for **privacy, freedom of expression**, and **security**, it also raises concerns about accountability and the potential for **illicit activities** to thrive without consequence. The challenge lies in balancing the

fundamental right to privacy with the need to prevent **harmful behavior** that anonymity can facilitate.

For **journalists**, **activists**, and **whistleblowers** working in **repressive regions**, anonymity is a vital tool that allows them to **expose corruption**, **challenge authority**, and **speak truth to power**. In these contexts, the ethical use of anonymity can be life-saving and essential to preserving **human rights**.

Ultimately, the ethical question of anonymity requires careful consideration of the **benefits** and **dangers** it presents. While anonymity can protect vulnerable individuals, it must also be recognized as a potential tool for abuse, making the **ethical governance** of online anonymity a key issue for policymakers, law enforcement, and society at large.

CHAPTER 19

Dark Web and Digital Rights

How the Dark Web Relates to Broader Digital Rights Issues

The **Dark Web** is deeply connected to **digital rights** and has become a focal point in the ongoing global debate about privacy, **freedom of expression**, and **surveillance**. As governments and corporations increasingly monitor online activity, individuals are increasingly concerned about how their personal data is being collected and used. The Dark Web offers a unique perspective on these concerns, as it provides a space where users can engage in **anonymous communication** and access information **without surveillance**.

1. Privacy as a Digital Right

The **right to privacy** is one of the most fundamental **digital rights**, and it is increasingly under threat in the **modern digital landscape**. **Data mining, social media tracking**, and **government surveillance** have made it difficult for individuals to maintain their **personal privacy** online. On the Dark Web, tools like **Tor** and **I2P** provide a way for individuals to **protect their anonymity**, hide their location, and prevent their personal data from being collected.

- **Digital Surveillance**: As **surveillance technology** becomes more sophisticated, **governments** and **corporations** can track nearly every action individuals take online. From **location tracking** via mobile devices to the collection of **personal browsing data**, digital surveillance has become pervasive. The Dark Web, in contrast, provides a **refuge** for individuals seeking to keep their online activities private, away from prying eyes.

- **Encryption and Anonymity**: Services like **Tor** and **I2P** allow users to **obscure their digital footprint** by routing internet traffic through encrypted channels. These tools enable individuals to communicate securely, browse anonymously, and **avoid online surveillance**—critical features for those who wish to **protect their digital rights**.

2. Freedom of Expression in the Digital Age

The **right to free speech** is also increasingly challenged in the digital world. In many countries, governments have tightened **censorship** and restricted access to online information. The Dark Web provides a space where individuals can express their opinions freely, **without fear of government censorship** or reprisal.

- **Censorship Resistance**: In **authoritarian** or **repressive regimes**, online speech is often closely monitored. Governments frequently block access to websites or platforms that host content deemed "subversive" or "illegal," such as **news outlets** or **human rights forums**. The Dark Web allows individuals in these countries to **circumvent censorship** and access information or share ideas without fear of being arrested or persecuted.

- **Political Activism**: For **activists** and **journalists** working in repressive environments, the Dark Web offers a **secure** and **anonymous** platform for organizing, sharing news, and advocating for political change. These platforms allow individuals to engage in **free speech** without the threat of being tracked, identified, or silenced.

The Ongoing Debate About the Need for Privacy vs. the Dangers of Anonymity

The debate over the **need for privacy** versus the **dangers of anonymity** is one of the most contentious issues when it comes to digital rights. While privacy advocates argue that anonymity is necessary to protect civil liberties, others believe that excessive anonymity on the internet can facilitate **illegal activities** and **harmful behavior**.

1. Privacy as a Protection Against Abuse

The need for **privacy** is often tied to the broader principle of **human dignity** and **freedom**. Without privacy, individuals can be subject to **exploitation**, **identity theft**, or **unwanted surveillance**. Digital privacy helps protect people from **corporate control**, **political repression**, and **unjust discrimination**.

- **Safeguarding Personal Data**: As individuals share more information online, **identity theft** and **data breaches** become more prevalent. Anonymity on the Dark Web allows individuals to take control over their **personal information** and ensure that it is not

exploited by marketers, government agencies, or malicious actors.

- **Protection from Discrimination**: Anonymity can also protect individuals from discrimination based on their race, gender, sexual orientation, or political beliefs. In societies where marginalized groups are at risk of persecution, being able to remain **anonymous** online can be a **lifeline** that allows them to express themselves freely and seek help.

2. The Dangers of Anonymity

However, the other side of the argument focuses on the **dangers** of anonymity, particularly when it is used to shield illegal or harmful activities. While anonymity can be an essential tool for privacy and freedom of expression, it can also be misused by individuals who wish to engage in **cybercrime**, **fraud**, or **harassment**.

- **Enabling Illicit Activities**: The **Dark Web** has become a hotbed for **illegal trade**, including the sale of **drugs**, **weapons**, and **stolen data**. Anonymity allows these activities to flourish without the fear of law enforcement intervention. Some argue that by protecting **anonymity**, the Dark Web becomes a breeding ground for **criminal behavior**, and that the authorities should work to restrict it.

- **Cyberbullying and Harassment**: Anonymity can also be used to shield individuals engaging in **cyberbullying**, **hate speech**, or **identity theft**. While some believe anonymity protects freedom of speech, others argue that it can also be used to **harm** others, particularly vulnerable individuals.

3. Finding a Balance

The challenge lies in finding a balance between the **right to privacy** and the need for **security** and **accountability**. Anonymity should not be an excuse to shield illegal behavior, but it is equally important to preserve privacy and **free expression** for those who use it responsibly. This tension between privacy and security is at the heart of the ongoing debate about the ethical implications of the Dark Web.

Real-World Example: The Impact of Surveillance on Free Speech and How the Dark Web Provides a Haven

One of the most compelling real-world examples of how the Dark Web provides a **haven** for free speech in the face of **surveillance** is the story of **journalists** and **activists** in **authoritarian regimes**. In countries where **online censorship** is prevalent, the ability to speak out or access independent news sources can be life-threatening.

Example 1: The Role of the Dark Web in the Arab Spring

During the **Arab Spring** uprisings in 2010–2011, people living in countries like **Egypt, Tunisia**, and **Syria** used **anonymity** to coordinate protests and share information about the uprisings, bypassing government censorship and surveillance.

- **Bypassing Censorship**: In these countries, the governments attempted to **block social media** platforms like **Facebook** and **Twitter** to prevent people from organizing protests. Activists used **Tor** and other encryption tools to **access uncensored content** and communicate securely. The Dark Web became a **crucial tool** for maintaining **free speech** in the face of government surveillance and repression.

- **Journalists Protecting Sources**: Journalists covering the events relied on **secure communication tools** to protect their sources from surveillance. The Dark Web allowed them to **receive anonymous tips** and **leak confidential documents** without compromising their sources' safety.

Example 2: Whistleblowing on the Dark Web

Another example of the **Dark Web** protecting **free speech** and **privacy** is its use by **whistleblowers** to leak sensitive information about **government corruption**, **corporate malfeasance**, and **human rights violations**.

- **Edward Snowden and the NSA Leaks**: In 2013, **Edward Snowden** used **Tor** and other encrypted communication tools to **leak classified documents** about the **NSA's mass surveillance programs**. Snowden relied on **anonymity** to protect his identity as he communicated with journalists from **The Guardian** and **The Washington Post**, ensuring that his whistleblowing could not be traced back to him.

- **SecureDrop**: Platforms like **SecureDrop** allow **journalists** to receive anonymous tips and documents from whistleblowers. This platform ensures that sources can **safely leak information** without fear of retaliation. Whistleblowers rely on these tools to expose wrongdoing while maintaining their **privacy** and **security**.

Conclusion

The **Dark Web** is inextricably linked to the **broader debate about digital rights**, particularly concerning **privacy, free speech**, and **surveillance**. While the **Dark Web** has become a tool for **criminal activity**, it also serves as a crucial platform for **protecting digital rights, ensuring privacy**, and enabling **free expression**, especially in environments where **censorship** and **government surveillance** are rampant.

The ongoing debate about the need for **privacy** versus the **dangers of anonymity** is central to understanding the ethical implications of the Dark Web. While anonymity can be used to **protect individuals** and **uphold freedom of speech**, it can also be exploited by those who wish to **engage in illicit**

198

activities. As governments and organizations continue to balance these competing interests, it is essential to recognize the importance of **privacy** and **anonymity** as tools for safeguarding **digital rights** in a **hyper-surveilled** world.

CHAPTER 20

Balancing Law Enforcement and Privacy

How Law Enforcement Agencies Balance Fighting Cybercrime with Respecting Privacy

As cybercrime continues to grow and evolve, law enforcement agencies are increasingly focused on combatting illegal activities on the **Dark Web**, such as **drug trafficking, cybercrime, money laundering**, and **child exploitation**. However, these efforts to address crime often intersect with concerns about **privacy rights** and **civil liberties**. The challenge for law enforcement is to find an effective balance between **protecting society** from illegal activities and **respecting** individuals' **right to privacy**.

1. Law Enforcement's Role in the Digital Age

With the rise of the **Dark Web**, law enforcement agencies are faced with a new kind of **criminal landscape**—one that operates in **relative anonymity** and often beyond the jurisdiction of national law enforcement. Criminals use **encryption, pseudonymity**, and **cryptocurrency** to engage in illegal activities without leaving a trace. This complicates the work of law enforcement, which traditionally relied on more **tangible evidence** and **physical surveillance**.

However, the digital age also offers law enforcement agencies new tools for investigating and prosecuting crimes, such as **cyber surveillance**, **blockchain analysis**, and **data mining**. These tools can be used to track **online transactions**, monitor **Dark Web marketplaces**, and identify **suspected criminals**—all without directly violating the **privacy** of innocent individuals.

2. The Challenge of Protecting Privacy

The core dilemma for law enforcement is how to **intervene** in the **Dark Web** while still respecting the **privacy rights** of users who may not be engaging in illegal activities. **Encryption** and **anonymity tools** like **Tor** offer critical protections for individuals who need them, such as **journalists**, **whistleblowers**, and **activists** in repressive regimes. Law enforcement's efforts to track and disrupt criminal activity must be balanced with the protection of these **fundamental rights**.

- **Overreach and Civil Liberties**: Privacy advocates warn that overly aggressive surveillance techniques could infringe upon civil liberties and create a **surveillance state** where **personal freedoms** are compromised in the name of security. Excessive monitoring of the Dark Web could lead to **unwarranted invasions of privacy, unjustified arrests**, or the erosion of trust in online communication.

- **Targeted Enforcement**: Law enforcement agencies aim to target criminal activity without overreaching into areas where individuals have a legitimate right to privacy. The key is **proportionality**—ensuring that the level of intervention is appropriate for the level of threat posed by the criminal activity, while still protecting the privacy of innocent individuals.

The Global Legal Landscape Regarding the Dark Web

The **Dark Web** exists in a **global** and **borderless** environment, where jurisdictional boundaries are difficult to enforce. Criminals can operate from one country while targeting victims in another, making it challenging for law enforcement agencies to coordinate responses and enforce laws. The **global nature** of the Dark Web complicates efforts to combat crime, as different countries have **different laws** regarding **cybercrime**, **privacy**, and **surveillance**.

1. Varying Legal Frameworks

Each country has its own **legal framework** for handling cybercrime and online activities. Some nations, particularly those with **authoritarian regimes**, impose strict **censorship** and surveillance, while others prioritize **privacy rights** and **freedom of speech**. For example:

- **United States**: The **U.S.** has taken a **proactive approach** to combat Dark Web crime through agencies like the **FBI** and **DEA**. However, it also has laws in place that safeguard **digital rights**, such as the **Fourth Amendment**, which protects against unreasonable searches and seizures. The **U.S. government** has also supported **global cooperation** with agencies like **Europol** to tackle international Dark Web crime.

- **European Union**: The **EU** has stringent **privacy laws**, such as the **General Data Protection Regulation (GDPR)**, which restricts the collection and use of personal data. At the same time, European law enforcement agencies cooperate with global efforts to combat cybercrime through **Europol** and **Eurojust**.

- **China and Russia**: On the other end of the spectrum, **countries like China** and **Russia** maintain strict **internet censorship** laws and have expanded their **surveillance efforts**. In these countries, the government heavily monitors internet activity, limiting access to the Dark Web and restricting access to information that is deemed politically sensitive or subversive.

2. International Cooperation and Challenges

International cooperation is vital in tackling Dark Web crime due to its **cross-border** nature. Agencies like **Europol** and **Interpol** facilitate cooperation between law enforcement agencies across different jurisdictions. However, challenges remain, particularly in areas where countries do not have **extradition treaties** or where law enforcement agencies lack the resources or political will to target international criminal networks.

- **Harmonizing Laws**: One of the challenges of global law enforcement is the **lack of harmonization** between the laws of different countries. While one country may prioritize **privacy protection**, another might take a more aggressive stance toward **cybercrime** surveillance. This can create **jurisdictional challenges** when it comes to **prosecuting criminals** who operate across borders.

- **Cross-Border Data Sharing**: The **sharing of data** between countries is another issue. Some countries, especially those with **strong privacy protections**, may be hesitant to share information about individuals without proper **legal safeguards**. This can slow down international investigations and lead to inconsistent enforcement.

Real-World Example: The Clash Between Privacy Advocates and Law Enforcement in the Context of the Dark Web

A significant **real-world example** of the clash between **privacy advocates** and **law enforcement** regarding the Dark Web occurred during the investigation and takedown of **Silk Road**. Silk Road was a **Dark Web marketplace** that facilitated the sale of **illegal drugs**, **weapons**, and **stolen data**. The marketplace was shut down in 2013 by the **FBI** after an investigation into its activities, which culminated in the arrest of its creator, **Ross Ulbricht** (operating under the alias **Dread Pirate Roberts**).

The Law Enforcement Perspective

From the perspective of law enforcement, Silk Road was an illegal operation that needed to be shut down to prevent the trafficking of drugs and other illicit goods. The **FBI** tracked **Bitcoin transactions** and used **undercover operations** to infiltrate the marketplace. Ulbricht was arrested and charged with **money laundering, drug trafficking**, and **computer hacking**, leading to his conviction and life sentence in 2015.

The takedown of Silk Road was seen as a major victory for law enforcement in the battle against **Dark Web crime**. It also highlighted the capabilities of law enforcement agencies to use new technologies and investigative techniques to **trace illicit activities** on the Dark Web, even when criminals used **encryption** and **cryptocurrencies** to mask their activities.

The Privacy Advocate Perspective

From the perspective of **privacy advocates**, the takedown of Silk Road raised significant concerns about the **balance between privacy** and **security**. While Silk Road was

206

undoubtedly involved in **illegal activities**, the case also sparked debates about the **right to online privacy** and whether law enforcement should have the ability to monitor online activities to this extent.

- **Overreach of Government Power**: Privacy advocates argued that the takedown of Silk Road could set a **dangerous precedent** for **government overreach** into **digital spaces**. The concern was that law enforcement agencies could use the same methods to target individuals who are not involved in illegal activities but are simply seeking **anonymity** and **privacy** online.

- **Chilling Effect on Free Speech**: Another concern was the potential **chilling effect** that aggressive law enforcement actions could have on individuals who rely on the Dark Web for **freedom of expression**, particularly **journalists** and **whistleblowers**. The use of anonymity tools like **Tor** is essential for individuals living under repressive regimes, and privacy advocates warned that restricting these tools could infringe on basic **human rights**.

Conclusion

The issue of balancing **law enforcement** and **privacy** in the context of the Dark Web is a complex and ongoing debate. Law enforcement agencies must address the growing threats posed by **cybercrime** and **illegal activities** on the Dark Web while respecting the **privacy rights** of individuals who use the Dark Web for legitimate and ethical purposes.

As the **global legal landscape** continues to evolve, it is clear that **international cooperation** and the **harmonization of laws** will play a crucial role in combating Dark Web crime while safeguarding **digital rights**. The **Silk Road takedown** exemplifies the clash between **privacy** and **security**, highlighting the need for careful consideration of the implications of law enforcement actions on **digital freedom**. Ultimately, the balance between **privacy** and **security** will require ongoing dialogue, careful policy development, and consideration of the ethical implications of both **surveillance** and **anonymity** in the digital age.

CHAPTER 21

Emerging Threats on the Dark Web

What New Threats Are Emerging from the Dark Web?

The **Dark Web** has always been a breeding ground for illicit activities, but as technology evolves, so too do the threats that emerge from it. Cybercriminals are increasingly using more sophisticated tools and tactics to carry out their illegal activities, and these developments have led to the rise of **new threats** that are harder to detect, trace, and combat. Some of these emerging threats include **AI-powered cybercrimes, the sale of advanced malware**, and **the growing use of cryptocurrencies** for **money laundering**.

1. The Rise of AI-Powered Cybercrimes

One of the most concerning emerging threats on the Dark Web is the rise of **AI-powered cybercrimes**. Cybercriminals are increasingly leveraging **artificial intelligence** (AI), **machine learning**, and **automation** to enhance the effectiveness and scale of their attacks. AI and automation can help criminals carry out attacks more efficiently and with fewer resources, allowing them to target larger numbers of victims with greater precision.

- **AI in Malware Development**: Cybercriminals are using **machine learning** to develop **adaptive malware** that can learn from its environment and improve its ability to bypass security measures. Traditional malware would typically have a fixed set of instructions, but AI-powered malware can evolve in real time, making it more difficult to detect by traditional security software.

- **Automated Phishing Attacks**: **Phishing** is one of the most common forms of cybercrime on the Dark Web, but with the introduction of AI, cybercriminals can now automate and **personalize phishing attacks** on a massive scale. AI tools can analyze social media profiles, websites, and other publicly available information to craft **highly convincing phishing emails** that target individuals or companies with precision. This **personalized** approach greatly increases the likelihood that victims will fall for the scam.

- **Ransomware as a Service**: **AI-powered ransomware** is emerging as a new form of attack, where **machine learning** algorithms are used to adapt to different systems and encrypt data more efficiently. Some Dark Web marketplaces are now offering **ransomware-as-a-service** (RaaS), where criminals can use AI tools to automate and streamline ransomware attacks, making it easier for individuals with little technical expertise to launch sophisticated cyberattacks.

2. Advanced Malware and Exploit Kits

The Dark Web has long been home to the sale of **malware**, **exploits**, and **hacking tools**, but now cybercriminals are able to access and trade more advanced tools and kits that target **zero-day vulnerabilities** and exploit **sophisticated** security flaws.

- **Zero-Day Exploits**: **Zero-day vulnerabilities** are flaws in software or hardware that are unknown to the vendor and can be exploited by cybercriminals before they are patched. These vulnerabilities are often sold on Dark Web forums, where they can be used by hackers to gain unauthorized access to systems or steal data.

- **Exploit Kits**: Dark Web markets continue to sell **exploit kits** that allow criminals to target specific vulnerabilities in popular software or systems. With the **increased sophistication** of these kits, cybercriminals can now execute **complex attacks** on larger and more diverse targets, including **cloud infrastructure** and **enterprise systems**.

- **Targeted Attacks on Critical Infrastructure**: Another growing threat involves **targeted attacks** on critical infrastructure, including **power grids**, **financial institutions**, and **healthcare systems**. With more advanced malware tools, cybercriminals can breach even the most secure networks and disrupt critical services.

How Cybercriminals Are Evolving Their Tactics

As law enforcement agencies and cybersecurity professionals continue to improve their methods for combating cybercrime, cybercriminals are also evolving their tactics to stay one step ahead. The **Dark Web** remains a vital tool for these criminals, providing access to illegal services and products that allow them to carry out their operations.

212

1. The Use of Cryptocurrencies for Anonymity

The **widespread use of cryptocurrencies** like **Bitcoin**, **Monero**, and **Ethereum** on the Dark Web has made it easier for cybercriminals to **conduct transactions** while maintaining **anonymity**. Cryptocurrencies enable criminals to **avoid detection** and bypass traditional banking systems, which have increasingly robust fraud detection measures.

- **Monero and Privacy Coins**: **Monero** and other **privacy coins** are becoming increasingly popular for cybercriminals due to their **enhanced privacy features**. While Bitcoin transactions can be traced to some extent, Monero transactions are much harder to trace, making it a preferred option for **Dark Web transactions** related to **drug sales**, **illegal services**, and **money laundering**.

- **Cryptocurrency Laundering**: Cybercriminals are also increasingly using **cryptocurrency tumblers** and **mixers** to **launder their funds**. These services obfuscate the origin of cryptocurrency by mixing it with other users' funds, making it difficult for law enforcement agencies to trace the flow of illicit money.

2. Distributed Denial of Service (DDoS) Attacks

DDoS attacks have been a common tool for cybercriminals for years, but their **use has evolved** with the rise of the Dark Web. Today, DDoS attacks are not only used for disrupting websites but also as part of larger **extortion campaigns**.

- **DDoS-for-Hire Services**: Cybercriminals can purchase **DDoS-for-hire** services on the Dark Web, where attackers use botnets to flood websites with traffic, causing them to crash or become unavailable. These services are often used by cybercriminals to demand **ransom payments** from businesses or organizations to stop the attack.
- **Targeting Critical Infrastructure**: In some cases, DDoS attacks are used to disrupt critical infrastructure, such as **government systems**, **financial markets**, and **emergency services**, creating chaos and allowing attackers to steal sensitive information or engage in other illicit activities.

3. Exploiting the Internet of Things (IoT)

The **Internet of Things (IoT)** has become a major target for cybercriminals in recent years. As more devices become connected to the internet, vulnerabilities in these devices present new opportunities for hackers.

- **Hacking IoT Devices**: Cybercriminals are targeting **smart home devices**, **wearables**, and even **medical equipment** to access private data or launch **botnet attacks**. Many IoT devices have weak security, making them an attractive target for hackers looking to infiltrate networks or engage in **identity theft** and **data breaches**.

- **DDoS Attacks via IoT**: In 2016, the **Mirai botnet** demonstrated how IoT devices could be used to carry out massive DDoS attacks. The botnet was built by exploiting **insecure IoT devices**, such as cameras and routers, and was used to launch one of the largest DDoS attacks in history.

Real-World Example: The Rise of AI-Powered Cybercrimes and Its Connections to the Dark Web

A new and particularly concerning threat is the rise of **AI-powered cybercrimes**. Criminals are increasingly using **artificial intelligence** and **machine learning** to enhance the effectiveness of their attacks, and the **Dark Web** has become a marketplace for these advanced tools.

Example: The Use of AI in Malware Development

One real-world example of AI-powered cybercrime is the development of **adaptive malware** that uses machine learning to learn and evolve in real time. Traditional malware operates with a fixed set of instructions, but AI-driven malware can adapt to its environment, making it more difficult to detect and defend against.

- **AI-Powered Ransomware**: AI can also be used to create **smarter ransomware** that is better able to find and encrypt high-value files. This type of ransomware can learn which files are most valuable to a target (such as financial documents or intellectual property) and prioritize them for encryption.

- **Automated Phishing with AI**: AI has also been used to automate and **personalize phishing attacks**. By using machine learning algorithms, cybercriminals can craft highly convincing phishing emails that are tailored to the target's personal and professional information. These **AI-driven phishing attacks** are often **much more sophisticated** and difficult for users to recognize.

- **Dark Web Marketplace for AI Tools**: The Dark Web has become a hub for the sale and distribution of AI-powered cybercrime tools, where cybercriminals can buy **pre-built malware**, **AI algorithms**, and even **hacking kits** that incorporate artificial intelligence to automate and improve cyberattacks.

Conclusion

As technology advances, so too do the threats emerging from the **Dark Web**. AI-powered cybercrimes, **advanced malware**, and **cryptocurrency laundering** are just a few of the new challenges that law enforcement agencies face. Cybercriminals are increasingly using **artificial**

217

intelligence, **automation**, and **machine learning** to enhance their attacks and evade detection. At the same time, the **Dark Web** provides a marketplace for these emerging threats, making it easier for individuals with little technical expertise to carry out sophisticated cyberattacks.

The rise of AI in cybercrime is a particularly alarming development, as it allows criminals to carry out attacks more efficiently and on a larger scale. Law enforcement agencies will need to adapt to these emerging threats by developing new tools and strategies for combating cybercrime, while still respecting privacy and **civil liberties**. The **Dark Web** will continue to evolve, and so too must the methods used to combat the illegal activities taking place within it.

CHAPTER 22

The Impact of AI and Automation on the Dark Web

How AI Is Being Used on the Dark Web to Automate Attacks and Operations

The rise of **artificial intelligence** (AI) and **machine learning** (ML) has had a profound impact on how **cybercriminals** operate on the **Dark Web**. As these technologies become more sophisticated and accessible, cybercriminals are leveraging AI and automation to **streamline and scale** their illegal activities. AI is being used to enhance traditional attacks, automate complex processes, and allow cybercriminals to carry out operations that were previously time-consuming or beyond their capabilities.

1. Automation of Cyberattacks

AI-driven **automation** is transforming how cybercriminals conduct their operations on the Dark Web. Tasks that once required human intervention—such as scanning for vulnerabilities, exploiting weaknesses, and spreading malware—can now be done by **automated systems** powered by AI.

219

- **AI-Powered Malware**: AI and machine learning allow malware to evolve in real-time. Traditional malware had a fixed set of behaviors, but AI can make malware **adaptive**, meaning it can learn from its environment and **adjust** its behavior to evade detection. For example, an AI-driven virus might recognize and avoid certain **security software** or **firewalls**, making it harder for traditional security measures to stop it.

- **AI-Driven Vulnerability Scanning**: On the Dark Web, criminals often use AI to scan for **vulnerabilities** in websites, networks, and devices. AI algorithms can sift through large amounts of data and identify potential security flaws more quickly and efficiently than human hackers. This **automated scanning** can then be used to exploit the vulnerabilities for **data breaches, DDoS attacks**, or **system takeovers**.

- **Botnet Operations**: AI-powered **botnets** can perform tasks such as **distributed denial-of-service (DDoS)** attacks, **spamming**, and **credential stuffing** automatically. These botnets, which are networks of infected devices, are controlled by **malicious actors** and can be used to flood a website with traffic, bypass authentication measures, or steal data.

2. Enhancing and Streamlining Dark Web Operations

AI is also playing a critical role in improving the efficiency and effectiveness of **Dark Web operations**. Cybercriminals are using machine learning and AI-driven systems to enhance their **marketplaces**, **forging identities**, and **improving communication**.

- **Dark Web Marketplaces**: AI can help **Dark Web vendors** by automating product listings, pricing adjustments, and even communication with buyers. Chatbots powered by AI can engage with customers, answer questions, and process transactions, all without human involvement. This **automation** makes Dark Web markets more efficient and responsive, enabling them to scale operations without relying on manual labor.

- **Improved Anonymity**: AI can be used to **simulate legitimate online behavior**, making it harder for authorities to trace illegal activities. By mimicking the browsing patterns of ordinary users, cybercriminals can evade detection and **maintain their anonymity** for longer periods.

- **Automated Identity Forgery**: AI tools can also be used to **create fake identities** or **synthesize fake data** to facilitate fraud, identity theft, and financial crimes. Machine learning algorithms can analyze real-world data to generate fake documents, profiles, or accounts that are difficult to distinguish from legitimate ones.

The Potential for Machine Learning to Help Both Cybercriminals and Security Experts

While AI is primarily seen as a tool for cybercriminals, it also holds significant potential to assist **cybersecurity professionals** in defending against threats on the Dark Web. Machine learning and AI are being increasingly integrated into **security systems** and **cyber defense strategies** to help experts detect, predict, and respond to cyberattacks more effectively.

1. AI for Cybercriminals

As discussed, AI is helping cybercriminals by automating attacks, making them more adaptive, and expanding the scale of their operations. Some specific examples of AI-driven criminal activity on the Dark Web include:

- **Personalized Phishing Attacks**: AI-driven **phishing attacks** have become more sophisticated and personalized. By using **machine learning**, cybercriminals can **analyze publicly available data** (such as social media profiles, emails, and websites) to create highly convincing, targeted phishing emails. These emails may appear legitimate and tailored to the victim, significantly increasing the chances that the victim will fall for the scam.

- **Advanced Malware**: **Machine learning** can be used to make **malware** more effective by adapting it to its target environment. For example, AI-powered malware can scan a victim's system, learn its vulnerabilities, and use **adaptive techniques** to avoid detection by traditional antivirus software. This makes it harder for security systems to defend against attacks, as the malware evolves and becomes more sophisticated with each encounter.

- **Smart Hacking Tools**: Cybercriminals can use machine learning tools to predict the **weak points** in a target's infrastructure, craft **customized exploit kits**, and deploy them automatically. This **data-driven** approach allows for more efficient and widespread attacks, increasing the success rate of cybercriminal operations.

2. AI for Cybersecurity Experts

On the flip side, machine learning is an essential tool for **cybersecurity professionals** in defending against the evolving threats on the Dark Web. AI can be used to **detect anomalies**, **identify attack patterns**, and **predict potential threats** before they happen.

- **AI-Powered Threat Detection**: Machine learning algorithms can analyze vast amounts of data from network traffic, user behavior, and security logs to detect unusual patterns or anomalies that might indicate a cyberattack. By automating threat detection, AI can identify and respond to cyber threats faster than human analysts.

- **Predictive Security**: AI is capable of **predicting** potential vulnerabilities based on historical data, user activity, and known attack vectors. This can help cybersecurity experts proactively strengthen weak points in a system before attackers can exploit them.

- **Incident Response**: AI can automate **incident response** by triggering **automated defenses** when a threat is detected, such as isolating affected systems, blocking malicious traffic, or alerting security teams in real-time. This helps to reduce the response time and limit the damage caused by attacks.

- **Dark Web Monitoring**: Machine learning can also be used to monitor the **Dark Web** for **stolen data**, **vulnerabilities**, or **malicious activities**. By scanning Dark Web forums, marketplaces, and other platforms for signs of emerging threats, cybersecurity experts can stay one step ahead of cybercriminals and take action before a full-scale attack occurs.

Real-World Example: How AI-Driven Phishing Attacks Are Becoming More Common on the Dark Web

One of the most significant AI-driven threats emerging from the Dark Web is the **rise of AI-powered phishing attacks**. Phishing remains one of the most common forms of

cybercrime, but with AI, cybercriminals are taking it to the next level by automating the process and making their attacks more **targeted** and **personalized**.

Example: AI-Powered Phishing Kits

AI-powered phishing kits are being sold on the Dark Web, allowing cybercriminals to automate the creation and distribution of **highly convincing phishing emails**. These kits use machine learning algorithms to **scrape data** from publicly available sources, such as **social media profiles**, **company websites**, and **online databases**, in order to craft emails that are tailored to the individual recipient. The emails appear more **legitimate** and **personalized**, increasing the likelihood that the recipient will click on a malicious link or provide sensitive information.

- **Phishing Automation**: Instead of manually crafting phishing emails, cybercriminals can now use AI to generate **thousands of personalized phishing messages**. This automation increases the scale and speed at which cybercriminals can target potential victims, making traditional defense mechanisms like **email filters** less effective.

- **Machine Learning for Evasion**: In some cases, AI-driven phishing attacks can bypass common spam filters by continuously learning from previous attempts. The machine learning algorithms used in these attacks can analyze which emails were successful and adjust their tactics accordingly, making it harder for security systems to detect and block these attacks.

- **Credential Harvesting**: These AI-driven phishing campaigns are often designed to **harvest login credentials** for high-profile targets, such as employees of large corporations, **government agencies**, or **financial institutions**. Once attackers gain access to sensitive accounts, they can escalate their attack, steal data, or initiate further breaches.

Conclusion

The integration of **AI and machine learning** into the world of cybercrime is having a profound impact on the **Dark Web** and its ability to facilitate illegal activities. From **automated malware** to **AI-driven phishing attacks**, cybercriminals are using these technologies to make their operations more

efficient, **personalized**, and **scaleable**. The rise of AI-powered tools is not only making it more difficult for law enforcement and cybersecurity experts to combat cybercrime but also highlighting the growing sophistication of threats on the Dark Web.

However, AI also has a significant role to play in the defense against these emerging threats. By leveraging **machine learning**, **predictive security systems**, and **automated threat detection**, cybersecurity professionals can stay ahead of cybercriminals and safeguard against new forms of attack.

The **AI-driven transformation** of both **cybercrime** and **cybersecurity** emphasizes the need for continuous innovation, collaboration, and adaptation in order to secure the digital landscape, especially as the Dark Web continues to evolve as a **hub for illicit activities**.

CHAPTER 23

The Role of Blockchain in Dark Web Transactions

Exploring How Blockchain Technology Is Impacting Dark Web Transactions

Blockchain technology, initially popularized by cryptocurrencies like **Bitcoin**, has rapidly become an important tool for facilitating secure, decentralized, and **anonymous transactions** on the Dark Web. Blockchain's inherent features—such as **decentralization**, **immutability**, and **pseudonymity**—align closely with the goals of **cybercriminals** seeking to hide their activities and maintain privacy. This technology is reshaping how transactions are conducted on the Dark Web, enabling a **new wave of financial operations** that prioritize **privacy** and **security**.

1. Blockchain and the Dark Web: A Perfect Match

Blockchain is a **distributed ledger** that records transactions across many computers in a way that ensures the data is transparent and immutable. These characteristics make it an ideal tool for the **Dark Web**, where **privacy** and **anonymity** are paramount.

229

- **Pseudonymity**: When transactions are conducted using blockchain-based cryptocurrencies (such as **Bitcoin**, **Monero**, or **Ethereum**), the identities of the users are hidden behind **cryptographic keys** rather than personal information. This allows users to engage in **illicit activities** on the Dark Web, such as **drug trafficking**, **money laundering**, and **cybercrime**, without exposing their identities.

- **Decentralization**: Unlike traditional financial systems, which are centralized and controlled by banks or governments, blockchain networks operate in a **decentralized** manner. This decentralization means there is no single entity or authority that controls the system, making it more difficult for law enforcement to trace or freeze transactions. This provides criminals on the Dark Web with greater **freedom** and **security**.

2. Blockchain's Impact on Privacy and Security

Blockchain technology enhances both **privacy** and **security** on the Dark Web by allowing for **trustless transactions** that are difficult to trace, alter, or reverse.

- **Immutability**: Once a transaction is recorded on the blockchain, it cannot be changed or tampered with. This immutability provides an additional layer of **security** for Dark Web users, as it makes it harder for law enforcement or other entities to manipulate transaction records.

- **Cryptographic Security**: Blockchain transactions rely on **cryptographic techniques** to secure the identity of users and the integrity of transactions. These techniques make it nearly impossible for third parties to access sensitive data or alter transaction histories without detection.

The Rise of Decentralized Marketplaces

One of the most significant impacts of blockchain technology on the Dark Web has been the rise of **decentralized marketplaces**. These platforms allow buyers and sellers to trade goods and services without relying on a central authority, which can be vulnerable to shutdown or intervention by law enforcement.

231

1. What Are Decentralized Marketplaces?

Decentralized marketplaces are platforms where transactions occur directly between buyers and sellers, without the involvement of an intermediary. These marketplaces often leverage blockchain and other decentralized technologies to facilitate **anonymous transactions** and **peer-to-peer exchanges**.

- **No Central Authority**: Unlike traditional online marketplaces, which are run by centralized organizations, decentralized marketplaces operate on blockchain-based **peer-to-peer networks**. This eliminates the need for an intermediary, such as a bank or payment provider, and makes it harder for authorities to monitor or shut down operations.

- **Smart Contracts**: Many decentralized marketplaces use **smart contracts**, which are self-executing contracts with the terms directly written into code. These contracts automatically execute transactions once certain conditions are met, ensuring that buyers and sellers uphold their end of the agreement. This automation eliminates the need for trusted third parties and adds an extra layer of **security** to the process.

2. Blockchain's Role in Enhancing Market Efficiency

Blockchain technology also enhances the efficiency of decentralized marketplaces on the Dark Web by enabling **instant transactions, low fees**, and **borderless exchanges**.

- **Low Transaction Fees**: Blockchain transactions typically incur lower fees compared to traditional financial systems. This makes decentralized marketplaces more attractive to users, as it reduces the cost of buying and selling goods and services.

- **Instant Transactions**: Blockchain technology allows for **near-instant transactions**, which is crucial in marketplaces where time is of the essence. Sellers can quickly receive payment and buyers can immediately receive the goods or services they've purchased, creating a more seamless experience.

- **Global Reach**: Since blockchain operates independently of traditional financial institutions, decentralized marketplaces are not limited by **geographic borders**. This makes it easy for users around the world to participate in Dark Web markets without worrying about cross-border payment restrictions or currency conversions.

Real-World Example: How Blockchain Is Used to Create Anonymous and Untraceable Transactions

A key example of blockchain's use on the Dark Web is the role it plays in **anonymous** and **untraceable transactions**. Criminals on the Dark Web are increasingly using **privacy-centric cryptocurrencies** and **blockchain technology** to carry out transactions in ways that are difficult, if not impossible, to trace.

Example: Monero and Privacy Coins

While **Bitcoin** is often the cryptocurrency of choice on the Dark Web, it is not entirely **anonymous**. Bitcoin transactions are recorded on a public ledger, and while the identities of users are pseudonymous, the **transaction history** is visible to anyone who analyzes the blockchain. This makes it possible for **law enforcement** to trace Bitcoin transactions by associating wallet addresses with real-world identities.

In response to these concerns, **privacy coins** like **Monero** and **ZCash** have gained popularity on the Dark Web. These cryptocurrencies use advanced **cryptographic techniques** to conceal the identities of both buyers and sellers, as well as the **amounts** and **transaction history**. Monero, in particular, uses a combination of **ring signatures, stealth addresses**, and **confidential transactions** to provide **complete privacy** for its users.

- **Ring Signatures**: Ring signatures obscure the identity of the sender by mixing their transaction with others, making it impossible to determine which one is the actual sender. This ensures that the identity of the person making the transaction remains hidden.

- **Stealth Addresses**: Monero uses **stealth addresses** to make sure that the recipient of a transaction is also anonymous. Each transaction generates a one-time address, meaning that the recipient's actual address is never revealed on the blockchain.

- **Confidential Transactions**: Monero uses **confidential transactions** to hide the amount being transacted, ensuring that the value of the transaction is not publicly visible.

These privacy features make Monero and other privacy coins ideal for use on the Dark Web, where **anonymity** is a key priority. Buyers and sellers can engage in transactions with a high degree of **privacy**, knowing that their financial activities are protected from surveillance and analysis.

One of the most well-known examples of a **decentralized marketplace** using blockchain is **OpenBazaar**. OpenBazaar is a **peer-to-peer marketplace** that allows users to buy and sell goods directly with each other using **cryptocurrency**, without the need for a trusted intermediary. It uses blockchain technology to **secure transactions** and **maintain privacy**.

- **No Middleman**: OpenBazaar operates without a central authority, meaning there is no third party to enforce rules or regulate transactions. Instead, users interact directly with one another, using blockchain and **smart contracts** to govern the exchange process.
- **Bitcoin and Privacy Coins**: OpenBazaar supports **Bitcoin** and **privacy coins** like **Monero**, which helps ensure that transactions remain **anonymous** and **untraceable**.
- **Escrow and Arbitration**: Although there is no central authority overseeing transactions, OpenBazaar uses an **escrow system** and **arbitrators**

236

to resolve disputes between buyers and sellers, ensuring that both parties are protected from fraud.

Conclusion

Blockchain technology is playing a significant role in shaping how transactions occur on the Dark Web. By providing **decentralized** systems that offer enhanced **privacy** and **security**, blockchain is enabling cybercriminals to conduct transactions without fear of detection. This technology is fostering the rise of **decentralized marketplaces**, where buyers and sellers can engage in transactions more efficiently and anonymously than ever before.

However, blockchain's impact is not limited to criminal activities. Its applications in **privacy** and **security** are also being explored by legitimate users and organizations seeking to protect sensitive data. As the **Dark Web** continues to evolve, blockchain will remain a key player in both **illicit and legitimate transactions**, and it will be essential for law enforcement, cybersecurity experts, and policymakers to stay ahead of these developments to address the challenges and opportunities presented by this transformative technology.

CHAPTER 24

The Future of Law Enforcement on the Dark Web

How Authorities Are Evolving Their Tactics to Combat Dark Web Crime

As the **Dark Web** continues to evolve, so too must the tactics employed by law enforcement agencies to combat **cybercrime**. The anonymity and decentralized nature of the Dark Web present significant challenges for traditional investigative methods, but authorities are adapting by developing **new technologies**, **collaborative strategies**, and **innovative techniques** to stay ahead of cybercriminals.

1. Advanced Data Analytics and AI in Investigations

One of the major ways law enforcement is evolving its tactics is through the use of **advanced data analytics** and **artificial intelligence** (AI). These technologies help authorities analyze vast amounts of data more efficiently and identify criminal activity faster.

- **Blockchain Analysis**: Law enforcement agencies have increasingly turned to **blockchain analysis** to

239

trace transactions conducted via cryptocurrencies like **Bitcoin** and **Monero**. Using specialized tools, authorities can follow the flow of **illicit funds** across the blockchain and map out the networks involved in **Dark Web transactions**. This has helped identify **money laundering** schemes, **ransomware attacks**, and other illegal activities.

- **Artificial Intelligence (AI)**: AI and **machine learning** are being used to detect **anomalies** in **network traffic**, predict **cybercrime patterns**, and even automate parts of the investigative process. AI can also help analyze **Dark Web marketplaces**, identify key players, and flag suspicious transactions or activities. Over time, AI's ability to analyze **unstructured data**—such as images, videos, and encrypted messages—will become a key asset in investigating Dark Web crime.

- **Automation and Predictive Policing**: Law enforcement agencies are also integrating **predictive policing** techniques that use **historical data** to forecast future criminal activity. By identifying emerging threats or areas where criminal activities are likely to intensify, authorities can allocate resources more efficiently and take preemptive action.

2. Proactive Monitoring and Undercover Operations

As Dark Web crime becomes more sophisticated, authorities are also adapting their **surveillance** methods. One of the most significant developments has been the move towards **proactive monitoring** and **undercover operations** in Dark Web marketplaces and forums.

- **Undercover Agents and Operations**: Just as law enforcement infiltrates physical criminal networks, undercover agents are now increasingly involved in **Dark Web investigations**. These agents may pose as **buyers**, **sellers**, or even **administrators** on illegal marketplaces, gathering intelligence on criminal operations and identifying key actors within these networks. By integrating **real-time intelligence** with **digital surveillance**, law enforcement can disrupt operations before they escalate.

- **Dark Web Crawlers**: Similar to how search engines index the Surface Web, authorities are now using **Dark Web crawlers** to continuously monitor the activities on **hidden services** and **Dark Web**

forums. These tools help track down new marketplaces, identify suspicious activity, and monitor ongoing criminal operations in real-time.

- **Decryption and Hacking Tools**: Law enforcement agencies are also enhancing their capabilities to **decrypt** encrypted messages and **hack** into secure communications used by criminals. Governments are investing in **decryption software** and **cyber tools** that can break into **private Dark Web channels** and intercept communications that were previously out of reach.

The Future of International Cooperation in Policing the Dark Web

The global nature of the Dark Web means that tackling **Dark Web crime** requires **international cooperation** among law enforcement agencies. Criminals operating on the Dark Web can span multiple jurisdictions, often exploiting **gaps in legal frameworks** to evade prosecution. However, international cooperation is evolving to address these challenges.

1. Global Alliances and Shared Intelligence

Law enforcement agencies worldwide have been increasingly working together to combat **Dark Web crime**. Agencies like **Europol**, **Interpol**, and **FBI** share **intelligence** and conduct joint operations to tackle cross-border cybercrime. As Dark Web crime becomes more sophisticated and widespread, this collaboration will likely become even more integral to successful investigations.

- **Joint Task Forces**: **Europol's Cybercrime Centre** and **Interpol's Cybercrime Unit** play a critical role in coordinating efforts across jurisdictions. These organizations facilitate the exchange of intelligence, provide technical assistance, and help law enforcement agencies from different countries cooperate effectively on **large-scale operations**.

- **Cross-Border Investigations**: Many of the most high-profile Dark Web cases involve criminal operations that span several countries. For example, authorities in the **U.S.**, **Germany**, and the **Netherlands** often collaborate on large-scale investigations into **Dark Web drug trafficking** or **cybercrime rings**. The future will likely see **more seamless cooperation**, as laws evolve to better accommodate **international cybercrime investigations**.

2. Legal and Ethical Challenges

Despite the successes of international cooperation, there are significant **legal and ethical challenges** that may complicate these efforts. Differences in national laws regarding **data privacy**, **surveillance**, and **jurisdictional authority** can make it difficult for countries to cooperate effectively on Dark Web crime investigations.

- **Data Privacy Laws**: Countries in the **European Union** have strict **privacy laws** (e.g., **GDPR**) that protect individuals' rights to privacy. These laws can sometimes conflict with the need for law enforcement to access sensitive data for criminal investigations. Law enforcement agencies must balance the need to track down criminals with respect for **civil liberties**.

- **Jurisdictional Conflicts**: Cybercriminals on the Dark Web often operate across borders, making it difficult to determine which country has the legal authority to prosecute them. **Extradition** laws, **international treaties**, and **disputes over**

jurisdiction can slow down investigations and complicate efforts to bring criminals to justice.

3. Advancements in Legal Frameworks

To address these challenges, governments and international organizations are working to develop **unified frameworks** for **cybercrime laws** and **cross-border investigations**. New laws and treaties may be enacted to address the **unique characteristics of the Dark Web**, including the decentralized nature of the platform and the **pseudonymous identities** of criminals.

- **EU Cybersecurity Act**: The European Union's **Cybersecurity Act** (2019) is an example of how governments are beginning to create more comprehensive and unified **cybercrime regulations** that can facilitate **international cooperation**. As **cybercrime** continues to evolve, expect to see more international initiatives aimed at creating **harmonized legal frameworks** for **Dark Web policing**.

*Real-World Example: A Case Study on How the FBI Tracked Down
a Dark Web Criminal Network*

One of the most successful examples of international cooperation and the evolving tactics used by law enforcement to combat Dark Web crime is the takedown of **AlphaBay**—one of the largest and most notorious **Dark Web marketplaces**.

The AlphaBay Takedown

In **July 2017**, law enforcement agencies, including the **FBI**, **Europol**, and **the Dutch National Police**, successfully shut down **AlphaBay**, a **Dark Web marketplace** that facilitated the trade of illegal drugs, weapons, and other illicit goods. AlphaBay was often referred to as the "successor to Silk Road," and it had a massive user base, with hundreds of thousands of users engaging in illicit transactions.

- **How the FBI and International Authorities Got Involved**: The takedown was the result of an **undercover investigation** and **joint task force efforts** between international law enforcement agencies. The investigation began in **2014** when authorities started tracking **AlphaBay's** operations and monitoring user activity on the marketplace. The FBI used a variety of tools, including **undercover agents**, **data mining**, and **cryptocurrency analysis**, to trace transactions and gather evidence.

- **Tracking AlphaBay's Founder**: The investigation eventually led authorities to **Alexandre Cazes**, the founder of AlphaBay. Authorities tracked Cazes' activities across the **Dark Web**, including **Bitcoin transactions** and the **use of encryption**, which led them to his physical location in **Thailand**. Tragically, before authorities could arrest him, Cazes died under mysterious circumstances, an event that some speculate was a suicide.

- **The Aftermath and Impact**: The **shutdown of AlphaBay** marked a significant victory for law enforcement in the fight against **Dark Web crime**. The marketplace's closure resulted in the seizure of **millions of dollars in illicit funds** and the disruption of several large-scale illegal transactions. The takedown sent a message to other Dark Web operators that law enforcement agencies could successfully infiltrate and dismantle criminal networks operating on the Dark Web.

Conclusion

The fight against **Dark Web crime** is an ongoing battle that requires **evolving tactics**, **international cooperation**, and **legal reforms**. As cybercriminals continue to innovate and exploit new technologies, law enforcement agencies are adapting by leveraging **advanced data analytics**, **AI**, and **undercover operations** to stay ahead of these threats. International cooperation will remain essential in tackling cross-border **cybercrime** and ensuring that criminals operating on the Dark Web face justice.

The case of **AlphaBay** demonstrates how effective collaboration between agencies like the **FBI**, **Europol**, and other global law enforcement bodies can disrupt large-scale criminal operations. As the Dark Web continues to evolve, so too must the strategies and resources used by law enforcement to ensure that the **digital world** remains **safe**, **secure**, and **free from illicit activity**.

CHAPTER 25

How the Dark Web May Evolve

Predictions for the Future of the Dark Web

The **Dark Web** has been continuously evolving since its inception, driven by changes in technology, criminal behavior, and law enforcement efforts. As technology advances, the **Dark Web** is likely to undergo significant transformations that will shape its structure, user experience, and the types of activities that take place within it. Understanding the potential future of the Dark Web is critical for both law enforcement agencies working to combat crime and cybersecurity professionals aiming to stay ahead of emerging threats.

1. Increased Use of Decentralized Technologies

The future of the Dark Web may see the rise of even more **decentralized technologies** that make it harder for authorities to track and shut down illegal activities. Currently, platforms like **Tor** and **I2P** rely on centralized servers to route traffic and provide services. However, with the growing adoption of **blockchain** and other decentralized systems, the Dark Web could become more fragmented and harder to police.

- **Decentralized Marketplaces**: Decentralized **Dark Web marketplaces** are likely to become more prevalent, with **blockchain** technology at the forefront. These marketplaces would not be controlled by a single entity, making it much harder for law enforcement to shut them down. By using **peer-to-peer networks**, these platforms could allow users to engage in transactions without relying on a central server, thus reducing vulnerability to targeted raids.

- **Self-Hosting Services**: The future may also see an increase in **self-hosted services** on the Dark Web. Instead of relying on centralized infrastructure, users could host their own websites, forums, or marketplaces using **distributed networks**. This would make it significantly more difficult for authorities to track down or disrupt these services.

2. More Sophisticated and Private Cryptocurrencies

Cryptocurrency will likely continue to play a central role in Dark Web transactions, but as the legal and regulatory landscape evolves, **cryptocurrencies** themselves may evolve to become even more **private** and **secure**.

- **Privacy Coins**: **Monero**, **ZCash**, and other privacy-centric cryptocurrencies are likely to see widespread adoption, as they offer enhanced anonymity by obscuring transaction details, making it even harder for authorities to track transactions. As privacy concerns grow, new **privacy coins** could emerge, using cutting-edge cryptographic techniques to ensure that users can conduct business without revealing any identifiable information.

- **Decentralized Financial Systems**: With the rise of decentralized finance (DeFi), the Dark Web could begin to see **decentralized financial systems** that allow users to lend, borrow, and exchange cryptocurrencies without the need for centralized exchanges. These systems could help users launder funds and **facilitate illegal activities** while maintaining a higher level of privacy and anonymity.

3. Artificial Intelligence and Automation

Artificial intelligence (AI) and **machine learning** will likely continue to reshape Dark Web operations. While AI

251

has already been used by cybercriminals to automate attacks and adapt to new security measures, the **future** could see even more **advanced uses** for AI on the Dark Web.

- **AI-Powered Malware**: **AI-driven malware** may become more sophisticated, learning how to bypass security measures or adapt to different systems. Criminals could use AI to **automate malware development**, quickly deploying new forms of malicious software across the Dark Web. This would make it increasingly difficult for security experts to defend against emerging threats.

- **Personalized Phishing Attacks**: With **machine learning**, criminals could **automate** and **personalize phishing attacks** on a much larger scale, making them more convincing and effective. By scraping public data from social media platforms, AI could create highly **targeted** attacks that exploit individual vulnerabilities.

- **Dark Web Chatbots**: The future of the Dark Web may see the rise of **AI-powered chatbots** that facilitate communication and transactions between buyers and sellers. These bots could act as intermediaries, handling negotiations, resolving disputes, and processing payments, all without human involvement. This could significantly increase the efficiency and scalability of criminal operations.

How Emerging Technologies Might Reshape Dark Web Operations

The Dark Web is not isolated from the rapid pace of technological innovation. Emerging technologies have the potential to fundamentally reshape how the Dark Web operates, how criminals interact with each other, and how law enforcement tracks illegal activity.

1. Quantum Computing

Quantum computing represents one of the most significant **emerging technologies** with the potential to impact the future of the Dark Web, especially in terms of **encryption** and **cryptography**.

- **Breaking Traditional Encryption**: Quantum computers have the potential to break traditional encryption methods, such as **RSA** and **AES**, which are widely used to secure transactions on the Dark

Web. This could render current encryption techniques obsolete and leave many Dark Web services vulnerable to decryption by authorities or malicious actors with access to quantum computing power.

- **Post-Quantum Cryptography**: In response to the threat posed by quantum computing, there is growing interest in **post-quantum cryptography**—new encryption algorithms that are resistant to quantum attacks. The future of the Dark Web could involve a shift toward **quantum-resistant encryption** to ensure privacy and security, keeping pace with quantum advances.

- **AI and Quantum Synergy**: The combination of **AI** and **quantum computing** could lead to the development of even more sophisticated tools for both **cybercriminals** and **cybersecurity professionals**. Cybercriminals could leverage quantum computing to enhance the capabilities of AI-driven attacks, while law enforcement could use it to crack encrypted data at unprecedented speeds.

2. 5G and IoT

The proliferation of **5G networks** and the **Internet of Things (IoT)** is another technological shift that could reshape Dark Web operations.

- **IoT Exploits**: As more devices become connected to the internet, criminals may increasingly target **vulnerable IoT devices** for **botnet attacks**, data harvesting, and launching DDoS attacks. The Dark Web could see the rise of marketplaces dedicated to buying and selling **compromised IoT devices**.

- **5G and Enhanced Anonymity**: **5G networks** offer much faster data transmission speeds and lower latency, which could facilitate **real-time Dark Web transactions** and communication. This might allow criminals to operate more efficiently, conduct rapid transactions, and make their activities even harder to track.

Real-World Example: How the Rise of Quantum Computing Could Impact Dark Web Encryption

The potential of **quantum computing** to break current encryption standards poses a significant threat to **Dark Web security** and encryption protocols. To illustrate this, let's look at the future implications of quantum computing and how it could reshape the landscape for both cybercriminals and law enforcement.

Quantum Computing and the Break of RSA Encryption

Currently, most Dark Web marketplaces, forums, and **cryptocurrency exchanges** rely on **RSA encryption** to secure transactions and protect user identities. This encryption method is considered safe under current **classical computing** but would be vulnerable to a sufficiently powerful **quantum computer**.

- **The RSA Vulnerability**: RSA encryption relies on the difficulty of factoring large prime numbers. Classical computers struggle with this task, which is why RSA encryption has been widely used to secure communications. However, quantum computers use **Shor's algorithm**, which allows them to factor large numbers exponentially faster than classical computers. This could potentially allow a quantum computer to break RSA encryption in a fraction of the time.

- **The Dark Web Impact**: If quantum computing becomes widely available, it could **disrupt Dark Web encryption** by allowing **law enforcement** or **criminals with access to quantum technology** to **decrypt sensitive communications** and **track transactions** more easily. **Cryptocurrency exchanges**, **Dark Web marketplaces**, and **private forums** that rely on RSA encryption could face increased vulnerability.

Post-Quantum Cryptography Solutions

In anticipation of this potential threat, researchers are working on **post-quantum cryptography** solutions—new encryption algorithms that are resistant to the power of quantum computing. Once these algorithms are developed and implemented, the Dark Web may see a shift toward **quantum-resistant encryption** to safeguard transactions and communications.

- **Quantum-Resistant Coins**: Some cryptocurrencies, such as **Quantum Resistant Ledger (QRL)**, are already experimenting with **quantum-resistant protocols** that would ensure privacy and security even in a post-quantum world. The Dark Web may adopt these or similar solutions to continue protecting user anonymity.

Conclusion

The **Dark Web** is on the brink of major changes driven by emerging technologies. As AI, quantum computing, and decentralized systems evolve, they will have a profound impact on the nature of **Dark Web operations**, the **criminal economy**, and how law enforcement can counteract these threats. The rise of **quantum computing** represents a potential existential challenge for current **encryption standards**, which are vital for maintaining anonymity on the Dark Web.

However, as technology advances, so too will the **tools** and **strategies** used by both **cybercriminals** and **law enforcement**. The **future of the Dark Web** will likely be shaped by an ongoing cat-and-mouse game between **innovative cybercriminals** pushing the boundaries of technology and **security professionals** and **policymakers** developing new measures to combat evolving threats.

In the coming years, the **Dark Web** could become even more **decentralized, anonymous**, and **difficult to regulate**, presenting unique challenges for both **law enforcement** and **cybersecurity experts**. As these technologies continue to evolve, the key will be to develop a proactive and adaptive approach to **cybercrime**, ensuring that the digital space remains **secure** and **safe** for all users.

CHAPTER 26

How to Safely Navigate the Dark Web

A Practical Guide to Accessing the Dark Web Safely

The **Dark Web** can be a valuable resource for those seeking **privacy**, **freedom of expression**, or accessing information that is otherwise censored or restricted. However, due to its association with **illegal activities**, it's crucial to take extra precautions to ensure that you **protect your identity** and **remain secure** while browsing. Whether you're a **journalist**, **researcher**, or someone simply interested in exploring this hidden part of the internet, **safe navigation** is key to avoiding harm and protecting your data.

1. Install the Necessary Tools

To access the Dark Web, you need to use specialized software that can **route your internet traffic** through **encrypted networks** and **mask your identity**. The most popular tool for this is **Tor**.

- **Tor (The Onion Router)**: **Tor** is the most widely used tool for browsing the Dark Web. It is an **open-**

source software that uses a system of **relays** to anonymize your internet traffic, ensuring that your activities are **hidden** from prying eyes. When using Tor, your data is routed through several nodes, making it very difficult to trace the source of your internet connection.

- **How Tor Works**: Tor uses a process called **onion routing**. Your data is encrypted in layers (like an onion), and each relay in the network decrypts a layer, sending the traffic to the next node until it reaches its destination. This process ensures **anonymity** by obfuscating the origin of your traffic.

- **I2P (Invisible Internet Project)**: If you're looking for an alternative to Tor, **I2P** is another anonymous network that provides similar protections. While Tor is best known for accessing the Dark Web via **.onion** sites, **I2P** is optimized for **peer-to-peer communication** and internal websites within the I2P network, known as **.i2p sites**.

2. Use a VPN (Virtual Private Network)

While Tor provides significant anonymity, using a **VPN** in combination with Tor can add an extra layer of security by masking your IP address from your **internet service provider (ISP)**. A VPN will route your traffic through a secure server, hiding your real IP address and encrypting your internet connection before it enters the Tor network.

- **Choosing a VPN**: Choose a **no-log** VPN provider, meaning they do not store records of your browsing activities. This prevents any traceable data from being kept if law enforcement or other agencies request it. Additionally, avoid free VPN services, as they may log your data or compromise your security.
- **Double VPN**: Some users opt for **Double VPN** services, which route your traffic through two VPN servers. This provides added anonymity by adding another layer of encryption and masking your real IP address.

3. Harden Your Computer's Security

Before venturing onto the Dark Web, it's important to ensure that your device is **secure**. Cybercriminals often use the Dark Web to distribute **malware**, **spyware**, and other malicious software. Here are steps you can take to **protect your computer**:

- **Keep Software Updated**: Ensure that your operating system, web browser, and any other software you use are up to date with the latest security patches. Many **cyberattacks** exploit vulnerabilities in outdated software.

- **Install Antivirus Software**: Use reputable antivirus software to detect and block malicious files. While no solution is 100% foolproof, an updated antivirus program can provide an additional layer of protection against **malware** and **ransomware**.

- **Use a Separate Device (Optional)**: For an added layer of security, consider using a **dedicated device** for accessing the Dark Web. This can help minimize the risks of malware infecting your primary device and separating your activities on the Dark Web from those on the regular internet.

4. Practice Safe Browsing

When navigating the Dark Web, it's essential to **follow safe browsing practices** to ensure your privacy and security.

- **Stick to Trusted .onion Sites**: The Dark Web contains a large number of **unregulated websites**, some of which may be scams or riddled with malicious content. To protect yourself, always use **reliable sources** or curated lists of trusted Dark Web sites. Avoid clicking on **random links** or entering unknown websites.

- **Avoid Sharing Personal Information**: Never enter sensitive personal information, such as **your full name**, **address**, or **financial details**, on Dark Web websites. Anonymity is a key aspect of using the Dark Web, and exposing personal data can compromise your security.

- **Be Cautious with Downloads**: Be very cautious when downloading files from Dark Web websites, as they may contain **malware** or other malicious software. If you need to download something, ensure that you scan it with antivirus software before opening it.

- **Use Secure Communication Channels**: If you are communicating with others on the Dark Web, always use **encrypted messaging services** to protect your conversations. Tools like **ProtonMail** or **Tails** (a secure operating system) can be used to ensure that your communication remains private.

Tools and Techniques for Protecting Your Identity and Privacy

Maintaining **anonymity** and **privacy** while accessing the Dark Web is essential. Here are several tools and techniques you can use to protect your identity and stay secure:

1. Disposable Email Services

If you need to create an account on the Dark Web or communicate with someone, consider using a **disposable email service** such as **Guerrilla Mail** or **Mailinator**. These services allow you to create a temporary, anonymous email address that you can use without linking it to your personal identity.

- **Encryption**: For a higher level of privacy, use **ProtonMail** or **Tutanota**, both of which offer **end-to-end encrypted email** that ensures only the intended recipient can read your messages.

2. Using PGP (Pretty Good Privacy) Encryption

PGP encryption ensures that any files or communications you send are encrypted and cannot be read by unauthorized parties. This is particularly important when engaging in any exchanges on the Dark Web where **sensitive information** is involved.

- **GPG Tools**: Use **GPG (GNU Privacy Guard)** or other tools to encrypt and decrypt your communications. Always use **strong passwords** and avoid sharing encryption keys with anyone unless absolutely necessary.

3. The Importance of a Secure Operating System: Tails

For ultimate privacy and security, you may want to use a **live operating system** like **Tails**, which is designed to protect your anonymity while browsing the internet.

- **Tails**: Tails is a security-focused operating system that routes all internet traffic through the **Tor network** and ensures that no traces of your activity are left behind. It can be run directly from a USB stick, leaving no traces on the host computer once you shut it down.

Real-World Example: How a Researcher Accessed the Dark Web for Academic Purposes While Maintaining Security

Let's explore the real-world case of an **academic researcher** who needed to access the Dark Web for a research project, while ensuring their **security** and **anonymity**. This example will highlight the steps they took to safely navigate the Dark Web while safeguarding their identity.

Case Study: Researcher Exploring Cybersecurity Trends on the Dark Web

Dr. Emily Greene, a researcher specializing in **cybersecurity** and **privacy** studies, needed to access the Dark Web to analyze **cybercrime trends**, monitor **Dark Web marketplaces**, and understand how **illicit activities** are evolving in the digital underground. Emily was committed to maintaining both her **professional ethics** and **personal security** during the research process.

- **Tor and VPN**: Emily started by using **Tor** to anonymize her connection, followed by a **VPN** to further obfuscate her IP address and avoid any exposure from her **internet service provider (ISP)**. She used a **no-log VPN** that promised not to store any data related to her browsing activity.
- **Device Security**: To ensure her **research did not compromise her personal data**, Emily used a **dedicated laptop** that she reserved solely for accessing the Dark Web. She installed the latest **antivirus software** and ensured her system was

regularly updated to minimize the risk of malware infections.

- **Privacy and Communication**: Emily used **ProtonMail** for encrypted email communication and **Tails** as her operating system for additional **data security**. This ensured that even if her laptop was compromised, there would be no trace of her activities once the system was powered off.

- **Safe Browsing**: Emily adhered to strict protocols when browsing the Dark Web, visiting only well-known and reputable websites. She used curated lists of **safe** and **academic-oriented** Dark Web resources to avoid risky sites.

- **Ethical Considerations**: Throughout her research, Emily remained conscious of the **ethical implications** of exploring the Dark Web, ensuring that she did not engage in illegal activities or interact with illicit markets. She used her findings purely for academic and **cybersecurity awareness** purposes.

Conclusion

Navigating the **Dark Web** safely requires careful planning, awareness, and the use of the right tools to protect your identity and privacy. By following best practices for **secure browsing**, using **encryption**, and employing **dedicated devices**, you can explore this hidden part of the internet without compromising your security. For researchers, journalists, or anyone seeking privacy online, it's crucial to understand the **risks** and take proactive steps to mitigate them.

As the Dark Web continues to grow and evolve, ensuring **anonymity** and **data security** will remain paramount. By using technologies like **Tor, VPNs, PGP encryption**, and **secure operating systems**, you can safely navigate the Dark Web while maintaining your privacy and protecting yourself from the potential dangers that lurk in the digital shadows.

CHAPTER 27

Staying Secure on the Dark Web

Best Practices for Staying Secure While Browsing the Dark Web

Navigating the **Dark Web** requires vigilance, preparation, and knowledge to ensure your safety and privacy. Due to its association with illegal activities, cybercrime, and the potential for harmful content, it's critical to take extra precautions when exploring this hidden side of the internet. Here are several best practices to follow to protect yourself and stay secure while browsing the Dark Web.

1. Use Tor or I2P to Access the Dark Web

To maintain **anonymity**, the most important step is to access the Dark Web through a specialized tool like **Tor** or **I2P**.

- **Tor**: Tor is the most commonly used tool for accessing the Dark Web. It provides **pseudonymous browsing** by routing your traffic through a series of **encrypted nodes**. This makes it difficult to trace your IP address and ensures that your browsing activity is anonymous. However, it's important to use Tor **correctly** to avoid potential security risks.

- **I2P**: If you want an alternative to Tor, I2P offers a similar anonymous network, optimized for peer-to-peer communication within the I2P network. It's often used for Dark Web services that do not rely on Tor's **.onion** domains.

2. Use a Virtual Private Network (VPN)

A **VPN** adds an additional layer of security by masking your real IP address. While Tor and I2P provide anonymity, using a **VPN** helps ensure that even your internet service provider (ISP) cannot see that you're using Tor or accessing the Dark Web. It also makes it harder for attackers or surveillance entities to pinpoint your location.

- **No-Log VPN**: Choose a reputable VPN that has a **no-log** policy, meaning they don't store any records of your internet activity. This ensures that even if law enforcement or other agencies request data, no information can be provided about your browsing habits.
- **VPN + Tor**: For enhanced security, some people use both Tor and a VPN. However, this requires careful setup. If you use a VPN with Tor, connect to the VPN

first (before using Tor), so your ISP cannot track your Tor usage.

3. Avoid Using Personal Information

One of the most important things to remember while navigating the Dark Web is to **never use personal information**.

- **Use Aliases**: When creating accounts on Dark Web services or marketplaces, use **pseudonyms** and **temporary email addresses**. This ensures that your real identity remains hidden.
- **Anonymous Payment Methods**: Avoid using traditional **credit cards** or **bank transfers**, which can link your purchases to your identity. Instead, use **cryptocurrencies** like **Bitcoin** or **Monero**, which offer varying degrees of anonymity and are commonly used for transactions on the Dark Web.

4. Be Cautious with Downloads

The Dark Web is rife with **malicious software**, **malware**, and **viruses**. Many websites may offer files that, when downloaded, will infect your system with harmful code.

- **Antivirus Software**: Always have updated **antivirus software** running while browsing the Dark Web. Even if you are cautious about downloads, malware can still sneak through if your defenses aren't up to date.

- **Scan Downloads**: Use trusted **sandboxing** tools to isolate any downloaded files from your main system. Additionally, you can use **virus scanning services** like **VirusTotal** to check files for potential threats before opening them.

5. Stay Away from Dangerous Websites

The Dark Web hosts a wide range of content, some of which can be dangerous, malicious, or illegal. While some areas of the Dark Web are relatively safe, others are rife with scams, illegal activities, and malware.

- **Stick to Reputable Sites**: Stick to well-known and trusted **.onion sites** that are frequently recommended by trusted sources or curated lists. Avoid clicking on **random links** or visiting sites you've never heard of, as many Dark Web websites are created specifically to **steal information** or **distribute malware**.

273

- **Be Cautious of Offers**: If a deal sounds **too good to be true**, it likely is. Be skeptical of overly generous offers for **illegal goods**, **services**, or **high-priced products**. Many Dark Web scammers offer fraudulent services or fake products to steal money or data.

6. Use Secure Communication Channels

When interacting with others on the Dark Web, it's important to use **secure communication tools** that protect your identity and ensure your conversations are private.

- **PGP Encryption**: Use **Pretty Good Privacy (PGP)** encryption to securely encrypt your messages. PGP ensures that only the intended recipient can read your messages, preventing anyone from intercepting and accessing sensitive communication.
- **Encrypted Messaging Apps**: Use **secure messaging apps** that provide end-to-end encryption, such as **Signal** or **ProtonMail**, for any communication related to Dark Web transactions or interactions.

How to Protect Yourself from Scams, Hacking, and Malware

While the Dark Web can offer a range of services and products, it is also home to a vast number of scams, hacking attempts, and malware distribution. Protecting yourself from these threats is essential.

1. Scams and Fraudulent Marketplaces

The Dark Web is notorious for scams that target both buyers and sellers.

- **Research Before Engaging**: Take the time to research the **marketplace**, **vendor**, or **service** before purchasing anything. Look for user reviews or feedback on trusted Dark Web forums and marketplaces. If you see any red flags, such as **negative reviews** or **unverifiable information**, it's best to avoid that marketplace.

- **Escrow Services**: Many marketplaces offer **escrow services**, which hold funds in trust until both parties fulfill the transaction. This ensures that the buyer receives the product and the seller receives payment before the transaction is completed. Always use

escrow services to minimize the risk of being scammed.

2. Hacking and Phishing Attempts

Phishing attacks and attempts to steal your credentials are common on the Dark Web. These attacks can trick you into revealing personal information or providing access to your accounts.

- **Avoid Clicking Suspicious Links**: Never click on unsolicited links, especially those that promise deals, **free goods**, or **exclusive offers**. These links could be part of a **phishing** scam designed to steal your information or infect your device with malware.

- **Two-Factor Authentication (2FA)**: Whenever possible, enable **two-factor authentication (2FA)** on your accounts. This adds an additional layer of security by requiring a second method of authentication (such as a code sent to your phone) in addition to your password.

3. Malware and Ransomware

The Dark Web is home to various **malware** and **ransomware** operators, making it essential to ensure your security measures are up to par.

- **Use a Dedicated Virtual Machine**: For additional security, consider running a **virtual machine (VM)** to access the Dark Web. A VM isolates your activity from the rest of your system, preventing any malware from affecting your main operating system.

- **Backup Your Data**: To protect against **ransomware attacks**, always have an up-to-date **backup** of important files stored in a **secure** and **offline** location. In the event of a ransomware attack, you'll have a way to restore your data without paying the ransom.

Real-World Example: Lessons Learned from a Dark Web Security Breach and How to Avoid Similar Mistakes

To illustrate the importance of secure practices on the Dark Web, let's look at a real-world example of a **security breach** and the lessons learned.

Example: The Case of a Researcher's Breach

In 2016, a well-known **cybersecurity researcher**, who was conducting an investigation into Dark Web marketplaces, fell victim to a **malware attack** while accessing a **suspicious Dark Web site**. The researcher had neglected to use a **VPN** alongside **Tor** and downloaded an **infected file** that appeared to be an **encrypted research report**.

- **Lesson 1: Always Use a VPN**: One of the key mistakes was not using a VPN in conjunction with Tor. The researcher's IP address was exposed, and hackers were able to trace their activity. This led to a breach of **personal data** and the unauthorized access to their **research notes**.

- **Lesson 2: Be Cautious with Downloads**: The infected file contained **malware** that gave hackers remote access to the researcher's computer. This malware allowed the hackers to steal valuable data. The lesson here is never to download files from unknown sources and always scan them with antivirus software before opening.

- **Lesson 3: Regular Backups and Encryption**: The researcher did not have an encrypted **backup** of their work, and their sensitive research was lost. In the future, it is recommended to **back up** important files regularly and encrypt any sensitive data stored on the computer.

This breach serves as a stark reminder of the risks of accessing the Dark Web without proper security protocols. By following the **best practices** outlined above, you can greatly reduce the chances of falling victim to similar attacks.

Conclusion

Staying secure while navigating the **Dark Web** requires careful planning, the use of security tools, and the implementation of best practices to protect your identity, privacy, and data. By using **Tor** or **I2P**, employing a **VPN**, keeping your device secure, and being cautious about downloads and communication, you can significantly reduce the risk of encountering scams, malware, and hacking attempts.

The **lessons learned** from real-world breaches, such as the researcher's case, emphasize the importance of **due diligence** and **caution** when exploring this hidden part of the internet. Always stay vigilant, and make security a priority to ensure that your **Dark Web experience** remains **safe** and **secure**.